PHILIP SHERRARD: THE UNIFYING VISION

Philip Sherrard

Philip Sherrard:
The Unifying Vision

Martin Corner

Oxford Publishing Services

Published in 2025 by

Oxford Publishing Services
34 Warnborough Road
Oxford, OX2 6JA
www.oxfordpublishingservices.com

ISBN: 978 1 0686789 4 3

Typeset in Berkeley Oldstyle by Oxford Publishing Services.

Cover image taken from a fresco by Aidan Hart,
www.aidanharticons.com, reproduced with kind permission.

Contents

Not there, not elsewhere, but now, but here, but this
stone, this shell, this flower, this tree, this sea,
each in possession of its own indestructible
beauty and being, in the deathless alleluia
of the windfall world.

'The Unveiling of the Bride', VI.

Preface

Philip Sherrard was many things: a poet, a soldier, a historian, a translator, a philosopher, a theologian and, in his later years, an environmentalist. His life, from 1922 to 1995, covered the central years of the twentieth century, years of war and its consequences, to which he responded in his own way: as the voice of an outsider, one who refused to be drawn into the assumptions of the mainstream, critical and prophetic in his analysis of the path that humanity was taking. An outsider he has largely remained; he is little spoken of, and his books, though in major libraries, have limited currency even in those areas where his thinking is most relevant.

Yet, though an outsider, he shared many of the defining experiences of the twentieth century. He was a soldier of the Second World War. His early experience of Greece was of post-war poverty and civil war. Emerging from that violence and conflict, he sensed a crisis in Western culture, which engaged him for most of his writing career. In his later years he was painfully aware of the betrayal of the environment. Nor, even as an outsider, was he without access to centres of the intellectual world. He was a fellow of St Antony's College, Oxford, and held a Guggenheim fellowship. He was twice assistant director of the British School of Archaeology in Athens. For eight years he lectured in the history of the Orthodox Church at King's College, London. His circle included Maurice Bowra, Patrick Leigh-Fermor, the poets Kathleen Raine and Peter Levi and the composer John Tavener. And there were his many literary connections in Greece, not least with George Seferis and Odysseus Elytis, both

Nobel Prize winners whose work (with Edmund Keeley) he translated.

But it still needs to be asked: why read Sherrard? The answer lies in the richness and range of his thinking. There is his historical analysis of the changes that took place in the Western mind in the late Middle Ages. There is his exploration of the theology of the Greek Fathers and its implications for the modern world. There is his critique of the cosmological systems offered by such as Pierre Teilhard de Chardin. There is his questioning of the limits to knowledge imposed by modern science. There is his effort to recover a true image of what it is to be human.

But behind those specific concerns there is a deep passion that suffuses all that Sherrard wrote: a passion for a unifying vision. This underlies his rejection, apparent from his earliest writing, of dualisms of every kind. It is there in his insistence that human beings are a single entity, body and spirit, at one with nature and with God. It is there in his search for a cosmological perspective that will embrace all being. It is there, too, in his recognition, in his later years, that any solution to the ecological crisis must go beyond physical practicalities to a transformed image of the human. He sees human beings in a conflict between fragmentation and transforming vision, between the discontinuities that shape our world and a moment, semi-mystical, when oppositions are resolved, when stone and flower and tree come together with feeling and thought and belief. His writing is an anatomy of conflict. But it is also a struggle to rediscover a point from which it is possible to see all being in unity.

That vision is, for Sherrard, intensely personal, in two important senses. It proceeds from the experience of living as a person, from what persons feel and perceive and know of themselves. But it is also personal in that what it reveals is personal: a cosmos in which the originating reality is itself person. Philosophically, Sherrard is a personalist in a world in which the prevailing models of being, both human and cosmological, are impersonal. To make the contrary point is, within contemporary intellectual culture, very difficult.

It involves at the outset a critique of foundational elements of Western thinking. It requires a re-examination of what counts as knowledge, of the limits of the knowable. Western society operates largely on the assumption that the knowable is defined by the methods of science; we can know, in any proper sense, only what science shows us. Much of the rest of human experience – feeling, belief, the perception of beauty – is relegated to the private realm of the subjective. Something can be said about them, but only as long as they too become objects of scientific enquiry. The methods of science work to objectify the human; we understand ourselves as biological objects, as psychological objects, as social objects. Sherrard works toward a recovery of personhood, of the human subject in all its participatory relationships.

He questions the domination of the Western mind by concept, by the conviction that conceptualisation is the only instrument of knowledge. Against that he points to those resources of human understanding, such as myth and symbol, that transcend concept. Myth leads him to tradition as a way of knowing. And as a poet as well as translator, Sherrard is alert to the power of poetry as a way of knowing.

To move beyond concept is for Sherrard the beginning of the vision of unity. Such a vision is more than a human strategy: it is metaphysical and theological. It is only from such a grounding that the fragmentation of human experience can be overcome. His critique of the contemporary world is more than a cultural critique: it starts and ends at the root of all things, the being of God. Sherrard is pervasively theological, fed at each point by his immersion in the writings of the Greek Fathers.

That makes him difficult; partly because the ideas are often difficult, but more because that is not a point from which contemporary culture likes to start. But Sherrard's conviction is that without that grounding nothing really changes; we are left, however skilfully we try to manage things, in a world of fragmentation. Sherrard's work asserts the necessity of theology. In a world that regards it as an outdated and unreal pursuit, he insists that the most basic human problems are irresolvable in any other terms.

To see the range and detail of Sherrard's references is to recognise that he drew on vast reading, from the Greek Fathers to Irish mythology to modern poetry across Europe. But though he held academic positions he was not an academic; his motivation and his methods were not those of a professional. Though his exposition of an issue may be complex and demanding, he wrote for a non-professional audience, for whoever had the concern and curiosity to attend. He belonged to a small group, those courageous enough to place difficult matters before a general audience.

A marker of that can be found in the reviews that he received. Most of them are to do with his translations, whether of modern Greek poetry or, in the later part of his life, of the Orthodox spiritual anthology, the Philokalia. His prose writing is very little noticed; after the 1970s, almost not at all. And the tone of the earlier reviews is revealing. *The Greek East and the Latin West* (1959) attracted attention from academic theologians, most of whom had difficulty with Sherrard's focus (theological, not historical) but found the book 'positive' or 'exciting', or even 'brilliant'. A typical response was 'stimulating but irritating'. He was not quite playing by the rules, but something important was happening. However, his later work did not go entirely unnoticed. The American environmentalist and novelist Wendell Berry and the poet Gary Snyder were both impressed by Sherrard's *The Rape of Man and Nature*. Berry described it as 'the best book I've read on Christianity and nature', and Snyder as 'really interesting and valuable'.[1]

---

1. *Distant Neighbors: Selected Letters of Wendell Berry and Gary Snyder*, ed. Chad Wriglesworth (Berkeley, CA: Counterpoint Press, 2014); letters of 6 and 18 September 1989. Other reviews are listed in the Bibliography.

PREFACE

Sherrard can be exciting because he makes unexpected inroads into habitual assumptions, but he can also be deliberately provocative. When he attacks modern science he is likely to be taken for an obscurantist, and when he questions the dominance of evolutionary models of thought he is likely to be placed alongside the flat-earthers. That he sometimes states his position with a degree of rhetorical violence does not always help him to be heard. Yet, such a response is implicit in what he is trying to do. He is questioning assumptions about ourselves and how we know the world, assumptions drawn from the culture in which we live and often so deep that they are not conscious. Sherrard is asking us to be aware of the conceptual underpinnings of our world, to recognise the often unseen equipment of the habitual mind.

The structure of this study follows the movement of Sherrard's mind across nearly fifty years. It is divided into two parts. For thirty years after his first arrival in Greece in 1946, his thinking was a response to what he met in Greece: the culture, the poetry, Orthodox Christianity. Throughout that period Greece provided him with a basis for his critique of the West, its cultural assumptions, its rationalism, its Christian tradition. His resources for that critique extend from Plato to the monastic life of Mount Athos and the civilisation of Byzantium. At every point, the presence of Greece is tangible.

That is the thread of the first part of this book. Then, in the mid-1970s, the emphases change. Sherrard's concern becomes broader, Greece is less directly present in his arguments. His search is now for an inclusive human image, one that will connect human self-understanding with an understanding of the cosmos, and Christianity is part of that. Those preoccupations, anthropological, cosmological and theological, link the last twenty years of his writing.

The book opens, though, with a prologue looking at his very earliest writing, the poetry he wrote during and immediately after the Second World War. The experiences reflected in that poetry are his starting point. His lifelong effort to reach a secure image of the human, one that offered an adequate vision of the full expanse of human life, began in the nullity and despair of those years. It was from that darkness that his search for light began.

Acknowledgements

This book grew out of a gradual accumulation of Philip Sherrard's writing over a period of at least thirty years, beginning with his translations and then, as curiosity grew, his prose works. What sparked my curiosity was Sherrard's intellectual ambition and his readiness to think from outside the general current; these were qualities that, after a working life in academia, impressed me as rare. He was interested in questions that interested me, in particular the West's disjunction from Christianity in the twentieth century, with non-clichéd interpretations of that pivotal historical phenomenon – and there was always, of course, his love of Greece.

So the point came when, convinced of Sherrard's interest and importance, I wanted to do something about it. Few seemed to know his name and fewer to have read him. So I set to work. But nothing could have happened without the help of those I was able to find who shared the same interest. I would like to thank all who have supported me with their encouragement and with information and corrections where they were needed. I have been very fortunate to have had contact with people who knew Philip Sherrard and who could help me. There are those who still live at Sherrard's chosen place, Katounia, and particularly Denise Sherrard, who from my first out-of-the-blue letter proposing this book has been warm and generous in her advice and hospitality, who has corrected errors of detail and supplied the portraits. I thank the iconographer Aidan Hart for allowing me to reproduce his work from the Church of the Protecting Veil at Katounia and for supplying the image on the front cover. Father Andrew Louth has been equally supportive reading drafts, offering corrections, and at an early stage supplying me with an unobtainable text without which the writing of this book would have been impossible. Another friend from Katounia, Andrew Watson, has contributed his memories of Philip Sherrard and his own quiet and encouraging wisdom. Then this study would not have seen the light of day without the help of friends of more than fifty years, Selina, Robin and Jason Cohen of Oxford Publishing Services, who have skilfully managed the technicalities and the production.

But most of all I thank my wife, Linda Corner, who – apart from the patience needed to live through my months of preoccupation with this book – has kept my feet on the ground, read drafts of the text, and helped me to make sense of much that, when I first wrote it, did not. Any clarity is largely due to her; what stays muddled is mine. So thanks, and (of course) my love.

December 2024

PART I

Greece and the West

Prologue: The War Poet

For a writer searching for some encompassing vision, Sherrard's starting-point was as unfavourable as might be imagined. Before his first contact with Greece in the late 1940s, he had undergone an experience that left a deep mark on him, and that was war. It was an experience of profound alienation, from humanity, from the natural world, and even from himself. The record of it is the poetry he wrote during those years. Reflected there is a world of disconnection, of the fragmentation of feeling and experience; a brutal reality that took him many years to overcome.

Sherrard's route to active service was through the Territorial Army, which he joined from Cambridge in July 1942. From reading history at Peterhouse, by the following year he was a commissioned second lieutenant in the Royal Artillery. After a period in Tunisia his unit took part in the invasion of Italy, and he witnessed the slow and bloody advance of the Allied armies northward through the peninsula, including the four-month battle at Monte Cassino. There, in the chaos of frustrated assaults and river-crossings, it was impossible not to be marked by conflict and ubiquitous death.

I

The war poems form a group of seventeen, which Sherrard published as the first section of his 1994 collection *In the Sign of the Rainbow*.[1]

---

1. 'Poems Written in Time of War', in Philip Sherrard, *In the Sign of the Rainbow* (London: The Anvil Press, 1994), pp. 11–33. Referred to subsequently as *Sign of the Rainbow*.

They are the earliest of his published writings. Written between 1940 and 1946, they convey the experience of a young man struggling with the shock of war. There is a deep estrangement from the world he had known as a child and from all natural relationships, under the inescapable violence of battle.

Sherrard's war poetry is, in its tone, very much that of British poetry of the Second World War: detailed, immediate to the situation, not aiming at the moral organ-notes of a Wilfred Owen a quarter of a century earlier. Of the poets of the earlier war, Sherrard is closest to Ivor Gurney; of his Second World War contemporaries, perhaps to Alun Lewis. Some of the poems appear to predate his active involvement. The first, probably written in Cambridge in 1940 and simply entitled 'The War', strikes a note reminiscent of Rupert Brooke in 1914: war as the cleanser of tired, habitual living:

> As if after long slumber the waters
> had freshly risen to cover
> the earth once again, and purify,
>
> since so much was necessary, our lives
> locked in their inherited dream,
> and make clean the roads throughout the land:
> so did the war uprise.[2]

But in the same poem the emphasis quickly changes to the power of war to overwhelm all natural living and make life unreal 'so that nothing we can do, or that has been done, /is more than shadow-play'.

That sense of loss dominates all the poems. Most strikingly there is estrangement from the natural world. In 'Spring', Sherrard registers its arrival, as vivid in time of war as it has ever been:

---

2. *Sign of the Rainbow*, p. 13.

Hark: it is spring again that conducts.
Hark: the arpeggios of cherry, flute
of the pink almond, the tremulous
violins of the swallow, minuet
of leaf and tendril, and now
the scherzo of red poppy by the wall.

But that music is now out of reach; war has come between:

O but no spring can make us forget
the horn and trumpet of war, no mere April chorus
drown the rifle's staccato or the stentorian
drum of the cannon.[3]

'Rest Camp' expresses the same estrangement. For a moment, war
seems distant:

From here the war seems very far away:
sheep trek the hills, the stone walls mount the lie
of land as far as the travelling eye
can see: trees by the billets dream all day.

But the landscape is veiled by the nearness of death:

... someone
who too long has heard of other people killed
looks for the last time at the sun-masked features –
the huts, the hills – mounts the truck, and alone
sets out upon the journey that he never willed.[4]

---

3. *Sign of the Rainbow*, p. 16.
4. *Sign of the Rainbow*, p. 18.

These poems communicate a world whose elements – flower, rock, road – are still present, but no longer connect. The result is an irony: the familiar is there but not there, undermined by the pressure of death. In 'Landfall', it is the human world that, for all its vividness, has surrendered its reality. It describes the arrival by sea of Sherrard's unit in the south of Italy; normal humanity can almost be touched, but then it is snatched away. As their transport enters the harbour everything is briefly alive and real:

> I think it was the Italians on the quay
> who made us laugh and broke our sadness down.
> Three of them were boys, an old man the fourth.
> Soldiers threw down cigarettes, for which
> they scrambled shamelessly. The boys were quick.

But that night, as he climbs the hill behind his encampment, estrangement returns:

> I felt again that fear in which we live
> and die, in which we build and sing and weep:
> that in the fight we lose all for which we fight.
> And then the hunger of our loss returned
> and broke the silent contours of the hills
> and turned to dust the sunken olive trees.[5]

In 'Point 508: The Apennines, Winter 1944', natural living seems unimaginable:

> Was life ever here? A priest's sanctuary?
> A child's playground? A garden where
> roses led to other dawns, kinder days?

---

5. *Sign of the Rainbow*, p. 23.

Now the landscape is strewn with the unreachably distant dead:

> Now the wind blows down the fevered valley:
> the empty mouths are stops where no music sounds.
> Death's mound and monument, still, locked,
> impenetrable. Here war's careless drift
> has left a gaping wound, a body
> whose torn flesh still bleeds: a world's warm face
> shattered among these gaunt and patient hills.[6]

The 'patient hills' suggest a strength that may survive all of this; and in the last section of the poem Sherrard reaches desperately for it:

> Lark-song, miraculous, unfettered,
> rings in the sun's face.
> Life-in-death songster, do you sing
> even in this place?

> If ever I am told (death's tale)
> 'here life's song is done',
> let your voice, bird, my prodigal,
> ring out in the sun.[7]

For the present, though, there is only the brutality, as in 'River-Crossing that Failed':

> Construct the scene yourself from what you've read:
> the houses by the bridge, the smoke, the well
> where they got the water, the usual smell

---

6. *Sign of the Rainbow*, p. 24.
7. *Sign of the Rainbow*, p. 25.

of bomb and shell-burst, the silly dead
looking so half-alive, the mess from mines
that blew off bits of leg.[8]

After the war, in the autumn of 1945, Sherrard revisited some
of those places, but the landscape was still so marked by death that
he could see nothing else. Memory, rather than offering healing distance, made battlefield experience more vivid. In 'The Apennines
Revisited: Autumn 1945' he remembers seeing death in battle:

Then death, the slump, the redhot needle piercing
the eyeball, the hands' grip relaxed as the scream
gutters; lastly, the head flung back, the idiot mouth
moving without syllable.[9]

In the ironically-titled 'The Living', where all the figures appear
dead, it is as though the landscape itself can speak only of death:

Lopsidedly, a wooden cross falls over a china pot
in which a few dead stalks of grass,
placed there by who knows what childishly loving hands
commemorate an archaic rite of death.
On the cross: 'Zum stillen Gedenken' ...
And here no tears to bless this wilderness.[10]

II

For Sherrard, that wilderness continued long after the end of
the war. In his first published collection of poems, *Orientation
and Descent*, which includes poems written between 1946 and

---

8. *Sign of the Rainbow*, p. 27.
9. *Sign of the Rainbow*, p. 30.
10. *Sign of the Rainbow*, p. 32.

1951, the shadow of war still hangs heavy.[11] The first poem, 'Letter', starts with a post-war picture of bomb-damaged buildings:

> Roofs of houses sink into the world of night.
> Street-lamps light the ruins: broken stairs, rafters
> bared by the winds of a recent storm.
> My room among the ruins, exposed to the storm that comes.

Again the world is a world of fragments. The poem has an addressee, but there is no sense of contact or communication. It is as though the currency of shared humanity has been exhausted:

> ... once again I am face to face with a life
> that is neither your life nor even my own, this
> dereliction, here, in a time of sadness ...

> We have wandered beyond the limits of our own identity,
> locked in a dream where nothing is recognised, where no one
> can say any longer what he was born for, for what he is
> dying.[12]

The alienation here is an inward alienation, the loss of oneself; of a man a crisis of his own being.

In the following poems Sherrard creates a sequence, a journey in which his dereliction is expressed as a struggle to an ambiguous destination, which is also a lost point of departure. It begins with a farewell:

---

11. Philip Sherrard, *Orientation and Descent: With Other Poems, 1946–1951* (Eton: Alden and Blackwell, 1953). Reprinted in *Sign of the Rainbow*, 1994.
12. *Sign of the Rainbow*, p. 37.

Friend, it is time to leave, each one of us as he can,
Each one of us into his solitude ...
We wait for the day when we set out
to follow
the way back to our origin.[13]

The way is hard. There are lost companions ('Those Who Were Lost'); there is an empty landscape ('Bulbarrow' and 'Black Country'); there is someone else, addressed as 'Guest', but again there is no contact. There are rooms and houses that feel like prisons, places that serve only to postpone some moment of decision:

what do we wait for, murmuring
our few thoughts in the language of a broken people?
We cower beneath windows that we dare not open,
in the darkness of an ancient fear, our shelters
these impoverished rooms, lodgings for a single night.[14]

But gradually the 'Descent' of the title begins. In poem 10, and echoing Eliot, the speaker begins to trace his way down:

Long descent to the seaboard through the midwinter pass
crouched against the headwind,
the eyes frozen,
the guide changing the route for reasons we never knew
and the wounded man, who is always with us,
silent under his pain
we kept to the by-ways, travelling mostly at night.[15]

---

13. *Sign of the Rainbow*, pp. 39–40.
14. *Sign of the Rainbow*, p. 47.
15. *Sign of the Rainbow*, p. 48.

This landscape is a place of exile; at points it is the devastated Europe of the post-war years. In poem 11, a frontier is reached:

> we wait
> among others who have no country,
> have no passports,
> who mumbling strange syllables try to remember where they
>   came from,
> among women who carry their few possessions on broken
>   carts.[16]

But the journey is not without hope. It is a journey back to some source, for which the image is the sea:

> Always a little closer
> we advance slowly down this trackless slope
> beyond the world that shutters the soul's window
>
> Always a little closer
> we grope our way
> through the steep gorge that leads back to the sea.[17]

Yet, all is sterile, deprived of the means of life. In poem 13, Sherrard takes an image directly from George Seferis, whom he was translating at this time: 'stumbling down the scarp like someone who cannot see, /lying up for hours by an empty cistern'.[18] Slowly some ground is gained. The loneliness, the isolation even from those who are sharing the journey, begins to soften in poem 15, 'He who was once the enemy is now the friend'.[19] In poem 17, there is at

---

16. *Sign of the Rainbow*, p. 50.
17. *Sign of the Rainbow*, p. 51.
18. The borrowing is from Seferis's poem of 1932, 'The Cistern'.
19. *Sign of the Rainbow*, p. 55.

least a memory of connection and love, but it is related less to a human figure than to night and darkness:

> Ark of midnight, when our life shared your love
> more soft than down your breath
> was felt upon the cheek, more cool
> than water from a rock your hand upon the forehead
> more gentle than the shape of leaf your look
> that left upon the heart
> a sweetness which we had not strength to utter.[20]

In the final poem (number 18), a destination of sorts is reached; the traveller has found his way to the sea. But there is little to find there, and ambiguity still prevails. Though there is something of a home-coming the isolation is not ended; there are companions, but they are not human. Again, the language and imagery are suggestive of Seferis:

> I have made my life in this small cave on the shore.
> All night my companion, the bird of elegy, his wound
> open to the stars, calls
> from his branch on the tree of sorrow.
> My only food the moonlight,
> my window a net …
> I reach my hands through the net into the silence
> Holding
> the cup which, however I try, I am not able to empty.[21]

The final image, suggestive of Christ in the garden of Gethsemane, hints at an unfinished sacrifice, a Golgotha journey that has yet to reach its end.

---

20. *Sign of the Rainbow*, p. 57.
21. *Sign of the Rainbow*, p. 58.

Orientation and Descent was Sherrard's first published work. It is not fully accomplished; the ambiguities of the text come often not from the experience itself, but from the effort, not always successful, to shape a language adequate to that experience. There seems to be a groping toward some mythic narrative that will properly contain the experience; the journey to the sea, Golgotha and the cup that cannot be avoided, help in that direction but remain remote from what is being described. How important an adequate myth was to Sherrard at this early stage is clear from his correspondence with the great facilitator of Greek writing, George Katsimbalis. On 9 March 1950, Sherrard wrote:

> The poetry of Greece is at its greatest at those times when the significance of the poem is so fused with the actual narrative that any separation is impossible, at those times, that is when the myth is the reality. And the loss of true vitality sets in at precisely the moment at which the significance begins to fall apart from the literal narrative, at the moment, that is, when the myth ceases to be the reality itself and becomes a myth of reality.[22]

This demand, for the unity of myth and meaning, underlies Sherrard's admiration for Seferis and Odysseus Elytis. At this stage, in his own poetry, Sherrard's myth is of the second kind, a myth that stands a little to the side of the reality.

Nevertheless, this collection of war poems has great power. It conveys a profound deracination, a severing of those links – to people, to places, to any familiar world – that make up the texture of human living. Aside from any verbal debt to Eliot, these poems are Sherrard's Waste Land. It is a land of fragments, devoid of

---

22. Initially published in 'The Light and the Blood', in Ari Sharon ed., *Arion* (Boston), 7 (1) 1999, pp. 63–71. Reprinted in *This Dialectic of Blood and Light*, p. 358.

participation in the life of nature or the lives of others, a place of absolute externality. Nowhere here is there the possibility of an inclusive vision; all that is to be seen are unrelated objects, the debris of a world in which all connections have failed. The voice that speaks from this place is alone, cut off from any mutuality of life. It was from this position that Sherrard began. The question that he had to face was how, in this desolation, could any connection to a living humanity be found?

1
Meetings

On 6 January 1949 Philip Sherrard wrote to George Seferis from London. In his letter he refers with unusual directness to his wartime experience:

> I was part of the war that happened in Italy – I sometimes put it that I was war in Italy, since that all became identical with a time of deep chaos and depression, even destruction, within myself. It was not until after that [that] I reached Greece – a meeting that still only begins to be made.[1]

The meetings had, in fact, been going on for almost three years. Sherrard arrived in Greece for the first time in March 1946. Still in the 1st Field Regiment of the Royal Artillery, he was part of the continuing presence of British forces that had arrived in Greece in late 1944 and would remain until 1947, with the aim of securing the stability of the Greek government following the German withdrawal in September 1944. A chance encounter led to his being given the task of arranging educational courses in Athens for British soldiers. He recounts the circumstance in a letter of 6 April 1946 to his friend Rupert Doone in London:

---

1. The letter and the correspondence with Seferis appear in Denise Sherrard (ed.) *This Dialectic of Blood and Light* (Limni, Evia, Greece: Denise Harvey Publisher, 2015 and 2023); these lines at p. 80. Referred to subsequently as *Blood and Light*.

I went down to the library at the British School to read Ovid.
… Only one other person in the room, so we had chats. He
is the boss of a historical course run at Athens for the army.
… Next he says he is going on release in a few days' time so
the course will close down. Why? Because there is no one to
carry on. Then ups me and says I know all about the Greeks
and their art. Really? Yes. So he phones through to the boss
and five minutes later I'm in an office and it's all arranged.[2]

He admitted to Doone that he did not know as much as he might
have implied; the work involved being 'up to all hours discovering
what I'm meant to know'. But his immersion in Greek history and
culture had begun.

There was another and personally more vital meeting. Looking
for translations of Seferis's poetry, Sherrard visited the Kaufmann
bookshop in Athens and was offered a copy of the French translation
by Robert Levesque.[3] The woman who offered him the book was
Anna Mirodia; they fell in love, and married in October 1946
following Sherrard's return to England. Anna was well educated, well-
read and fluent in three languages and in Ancient Greek. It was through
her that Sherrard learnt modern Greek so quickly and was able so
soon to begin his translations. He acknowledged that debt in his
letter of self-introduction to George Seferis, dated 21 February 1947.
Aware of the limitations of his command of the language, Sherrard
reassured Seferis: 'in this, my wife, who is Greek, will help me.'[4]

The alienation of the war years began to soften, and the ground
of it all was Greece itself. The country offered him a human world
quite unlike that in which he had grown up. In his letter to Seferis
of January 1949, he acknowledged that though his time in Greece

---

2. *Blood and Light*, p. 353.
3. Robert Levesque, *Séferis: choix de poèmes traduits et accompagnés du texte grec avec une préface* (Athens: 1945).
4. *Blood and Light*, p. 55.

had been short, the impact had been profound: 'my experience of Greece has been far more, and is, as I said, only at a beginning. It has meant an orientation.'[5] Its power can best be understood against the context of his earlier life:

> I can only say that at one time, not so long ago, I was in a state of deep perplexity. My background ... was that of the so-called enlightenment and rationality of the left-wing intellectual ... I was never in key with it, and it was part of my protest as it were which pushed me into the army as – terrible expression – an ordinary soldier: some need to embrace the most total opposite, the negative pole of existence perhaps, with no fear.[6]

The 'orientation' was to a language and a tradition from which the assumptions and attitudes of *entre deux guerres* England were absent. His sense of liberation comes across powerfully in some words that he wrote in 1980, in a tribute to George Katsimbalis after his death in 1978:

> If I were to try to assess the blessings I have been given in this life, I would surely single out as among the greatest my experience of Greek poetry and my friendships with some of the people involved in its making. I cannot imagine how impoverished my life might have been without that experience and without those friendships.[7]

What Greece offered him, and he seems to have sensed this almost immediately, was a different way of knowing himself and the world. He intuited the presence of a culture in which, for all the violence

---

5. *Blood and Light*, p. 80.
6. *Blood and Light*, p. 81.
7. *Blood and Light*, p. 365.

of war and civil war, there was still the possibility of an integrated sense of the world and of the human place in it.

That, for a war-scarred young man, was a toehold, a first glimpse of a possible point of re-entry. His desire to connect was intense: he spoke of a 'desire to absorb' that was 'inexhaustible',[8] and that made possible a sequence of encounters, not only with Greece itself but also with the poetry of George Seferis and the theology of St Symeon the 'New Theologian'. In the decade from 1946 to the publication of *The Marble Threshing Floor* in 1956, the meetings developed. At the same time and sometimes implicit but increasingly explicit, there emerged a critique of the norms of Western culture, of its image of the human.

How vital these encounters were for Sherrard is clear from that letter to Seferis of January 1949. After seeing the human capacity for brutality and destruction, he questioned what it was to be human at all. There must be a basis for the good, for a self-understanding that would make living once again possible. But the shadow of a world dominated by death continued to haunt him. As late as 1952, he wrote to Seferis:

> I've been in rather a bad mood these last weeks, a little close to the *selva oscura*, and have not been able to get things done as I wish. ... I need great watchfulness not to commit, spiritually speaking, suicide. There is that in us nowadays – a kind of nostalgia for death, a negative death, not that life-giving one: to give up the struggle.[9]

The problem was to find a connection between meaning and experience. The war had broken that connection. There was the outer world of fact and event, hideous often but often beautiful;

---

8. In the letter to Rupert Doone of 6 April 1946 (*Blood and Light*, p. 355).
9. *Blood and Light*, p. 245.

and there was the inner world of meaning and value, which seemed to float free in irrelevance. Yet, neither could be denied; it seemed as though one had to choose. In the letter of January, he tells Seferis of the pain of that conflict and hints at how Greece might offer a way through:

> In Athens, I thought I sensed a response to the need that I already possessed. ... What I call the need was to reconcile a love of creation which was an instinct of my psyche with a spiritual thirst which I believed then could only be satisfied with a denial of creation ... the 'way' for me is not to retreat before the objects of the outside world but to *cross over them* by an extension of consciousness, so that they are included within the spirit.[10]

What he glimpses is the possibility of a uniting vision, a mutuality of spirit with world and world with spirit; something that Sherrard sensed in Greek culture. Alienation might end with this 'extension of consciousness'. It was something of that kind that Sherrard found in Seferis's poetry: a way of uniting raw fact with the realm of meaning.

I

Sherrard had made his first approach to George Seferis in a letter of February 1947. Writing from England and quite unknown, he addressed himself to an older man already very distinguished, a leading poet and senior diplomat of a country with which, at that time, he had very limited acquaintance:

Dear Mr Seferis,
    While, last year, in Athens, I found your poems, translated into French: the Levesque translation. Even in a language not

---

10. 1949 *Blood and Light*, p. 82.

their own, their impact on me was great. ... Their importance is international. ... Unfortunately, there is, as far as I know, no English translation. With your permission, I should like to make translations of at least a few and to publish them. ... I know the inadequacies of my translation. ... Nevertheless, it is my consciousness of the worth of your poems ... that makes me seek your approval.[11]

The work of translation began and continued over the following year, with such speed that one year later, in February 1948, he was ready to read his translation of Seferis's 'Thrush' to his friend the poet Kathleen Raine.

As his letter of self-introduction shows, Seferis's poetry had an immediate and deeply personal appeal for Sherrard. But the first fruit of his engagement with the poetry seems to have been a sharpened sense of the crisis of Western culture. Both the appeal and the crisis are there in the earliest essay of Sherrard's to survive: one from 1948, entitled 'An Approach to the Poetry of George Seferis', which, again with considerable boldness, he sent to Seferis in the same year.[12]

The discussion compares Seferis with T. S. Eliot. Sherrard sees in both poets a recognition of the vacuity of the contemporary world. He paraphrases their shared unease:

In certain ages, of which our own is one, man seems to lose contact with the significance of things. Meaning, the *logos*, that is capable of revealing the true nature of reality and of shedding light upon the black world of phenomena is banished, sent into exile, and man finds himself in an inconsequent, meaningless, divided world of time and place. He

---

11. The letter was written from Bristol, where Sherrard was teaching in a school (*Blood and Light*, p. 54).
12. Seferis was at that time serving in the Greek embassy in Ankara (*Blood and Light*, pp. 56–74).

lives on the surface of things, and the depths of illumination that he possesses within himself are dried up.[13]

The division is clear: on the one hand there are phenomena, fragmentary and unrelated, the facts of the world, what Sherrard calls 'the surface of things'. On the other there is a void, an absence of the 'logos', which is both the deep order of being and its expression, which 'reveals the true nature of reality'. Without it, humanity is confined to surfaces and appearances. In such times of disconnection,

> man is called upon to make heroic efforts to re-unite and re-integrate the individual consciousness with the 'other world', the invisible, hidden world of meaning. He has to make these efforts first of all for himself. But if he is a poet, he will also be communicating to other people something of what such an integration involves.[14]

Sherrard's reaching for a uniting vision is already clear. Already it is an appeal for participation, not some cerebral explanation, but an integration of consciousness and world, and he glimpses that integration in Seferis. Eliot, on the other hand, though he attempts to integrate world and meaning, has, in Sherrard's view, never quite managed to close the gap. Speaking of *Four Quartets*, he suggests that the struggle has led Eliot 'to search for reality no longer in the external world but in another, a supernatural world'; the result is finally negative, an abandonment of the world of immediate experience. 'The natural world dies, we rid ourselves of the love of created beings, and devote our whole consciousness to the discovery of the other world.'[15]

---

13. *Blood and Light*, p. 58.
14. Ibid.
15. *Blood and Light*, p. 59.

Yet, there is such an 'other world'. There is the world of immediate experience, but there is also 'the invisible, hidden world of
meaning'; it is the task of the poet to bring them into one, to know
both without scanting either. In his comment on Eliot, Sherrard
already reveals his suspicion of a certain kind of otherworldliness,
one that negates or ignores actuality. For Sherrard, Seferis
successfully avoided falling into that trap. He found in his work an
integration of world and vision that he saw as the poet's proper
task.

Central was Seferis's relation to tradition and history, his rooting
in both. He had available, Sherrard felt, in a way that few Western
poets had, a living tradition, the life of Greece with its inheritance
of millennia. That gave his poetry resonance and depth: the broken
head of a statue could connect ancient and modern in a single
image. But such an image was more than a poetic device. It was a
way, simultaneously, of knowing both past and present; and, in a
world of divisive concepts, Sherrard saw in image and symbol the
possibility of a uniting vision.

Seferis's immersion in tradition was another way of knowing,
one that reached beyond concept. Tradition provided the poet
with a way of experiencing history, not as a set of facts external to
himself but as a way of knowing himself and the humanity that
his culture gave him. Sherrard makes a contrast. In Seferis's work
history is present in a way unfamiliar in the West, where history is
part of the world of fact and event, weighing on the individual life.
But he finds in Seferis

> quite another way in which history may be understood and
> this, far from enslaving and crushing man, opens the way to
> freedom. From this point of view history is an inner act of
> comprehension. ... [Man] possesses as it were a fourth
> dimension in which he is no longer a being conditioned from
> outside, but is able to condition himself from within; he is

able to be free. But to enter into that dimension requires a prodigious feat of creative memory.[16]

Externality is rejected; history is inner comprehension, an act of *anamnesis*, a recovery, not just of the past but of the self. The creative memory, most vividly exemplified in Seferis, enables him to participate in this collective recall, this shared identity, which, for Sherrard, speaks of a full humanity. Seferis makes such a recovery by drawing into present awareness a life that exceeds the life of the individual, but within which the individual can find completion. History, in this view, is a cumulative truth, a truth attained by participation in a common inheritance. When history is so understood, memory becomes 'the interior bond that connects the history of one's own spiritual development to the story of the world'; and in that there is recognition, 'the reflection of the history of one's own spirit in the past'.[17]

It is not that Sherrard takes Eliot to be unaware of the rooting of human consciousness in history. A poem like 'Little Gidding', looking back to the seventeenth century, strives to be faithful to that. But there remains something willed and external about Eliot's effort. Sherrard describes his work as 'primarily ascetic', dominated by a withdrawal that prevents him fully entering the historical moments to which he appeals. Seferis, in contrast, through his ability to inhabit his tradition, comes closer to the full recollection that draws together the totality of experience. That totality Sherrard calls 'the abyss of history' – an abyss not only because of its depth, but because to enter it is to abandon the individuality that cuts us off from the totality. Sherrard sees that relinquishing of the self in lines from 'Mythistorema':

Unto where will they carry me, these stones that sink into the years?

---

16. *Blood and Light*, p. 64.
17. *Blood and Light*, p. 66.

The sea, the sea, who will be able to empty it?
Bound to the rock that with suffering has become mine
I see the hands each morning signal to the vulture and to the
    falcon
I see the trees that breathe the black silence of the dead
And afterwards the smiles, immovable, of the statues.[18]

Seferis seems to be on the brink of a knowledge that is supremely worth attaining, but which never quite discloses itself. What it requires is the dissolution of individuality and an almost mystical entry into the physicality of the world. But that physicality is also the 'other world', 'the invisible, hidden world of meaning' that for us exists only in symbol:

The other world is incapable of exact definition and formulation, and must be approached intuitively. It can only be
mirrored in this world, since it has no concrete reality in the
way, for instance, that a stone has, or a tree. Indeed, this
world, the natural world, comes more and more to have existence not any longer in its own right but only as a symbol of
a hidden, invisible world.[19]

What begins for Sherrard in the language of poetry becomes, finally, a metaphysics.

In such ways, the Seferis essay of 1948 contains the germ of much of Sherrard's thinking. As well as an exploration of how poetry knows the world, there is the beginning of his critique of Western culture. At the heart of that critique, for Sherrard, stands the figure of Aristotle. Already in 1948 he points to Aristotle's influence as the source of that disjunction between world and

---

18. Seferis, 'Mythistorema', 20; Sherrard's 1948 translation, quoted in
    Blood and Light, p. 68.
19. *Blood and Light*, p. 62.

meaning that Seferis, in his poetry, is seeking to overcome. In his restriction of intelligible 'form' to material things, Aristotle has closed off access to what Sherrard has spoken of as 'a hidden, invisible world':

> The West has always tended to be dominated by the Aris-
> totelian conception of the relation of form to matter, and has
> therefore turned more readily to the organization and control
> of human affairs than to their transfiguration. At the same
> time, and partly in consequence, the separation of man from
> the other world is taken more for granted.[20]

Since form, which is the bearer of meaning and intelligibility, has no reality apart from its actualisation in specific entities, the 'other world' that he finds intuited in Seferis's poetry, the 'hidden world of meaning', becomes remote and unreal. Although Sherrard's full interpretation of that must await *The Greek East and the Latin West* a decade later, he is already prepared to give that relegation of the 'other world' a theological slant. Its effect is that God also becomes remote and unreal. As the world is more and more perceived in Aristotelian terms as self-sustaining, something else takes God's place, and that, Sherrard suggests, is morality. 'God' becomes little more than the validation of ethics, and finally a remote tyrant sup-pressing human living:

> Man's passive submission to the will of God, his obedience
> to the laws, and the importance of faith and works have been
> stressed more often than the need to realise the other life by
> his own creative effort. The *Imitatio* of Thomas à Kempis is
> perhaps the shining light of this attitude – a slavery and
> grovelling before God that strangles every potential

---

20. *Blood and Light*, p. 70.

superiority at birth, and results in the extolling of abject mediocrity and inferiority for its own sake.[21]

II

Sherrard's reference to Thomas à Kempis reveals his anger towards much in the Western Christian tradition. Two of the encounters of these years, with the painting of El Greco and the tenth-century Byzantine theologian St Symeon, develop that critique.

Sherrard's lecture on El Greco was delivered at Toledo in September 1950, while he was spending a summer in Spain.[22] The lecture is as much about Christianity as he has known it as it is about the painter. But there is no doubting the intense impression that El Greco made on him. For Sherrard, Domenikos Theotokopoulos parallels in paint Seferis's achievement in words: he opens a way of knowing the world, a way that is simultaneously mystical and material, that fuses physicality with vision. Just as Seferis had found a symbolic language that went beyond mere reference, so El Greco does not simply depict: he makes paint embody truth. Sherrard acknowledges the painter's mysticism: 'you may say that [the paintings] refer to man's inner world, that they are mystical works, speaking of that transcendent Godhead which dwells in a region beyond us, where our feet cannot tread, in the dazzling obscurity of secret silence.' All that is true. But the world in its vivid actuality is also there: 'where in the world of painting is nature – rocks, trees, flowers – given such a feeling of life, so that indeed it is like living tissue, like the flesh of a human body?'[23]

This unitary vision, this fusion of medium with meaning, is something Sherrard looks for in all his dealings with art. It is something he finds most powerfully in El Greco. But it is also what he finds lacking

<hr>

21. Ibid.
22. *Blood and Light*, 184–95. The lecture is dated 2 and 3 September 1950.
23. *Blood and Light*, p. 184.

26

in Western Christianity. There he sees a disjunction, between the medium of faith – its doctrinal formulations, its ethical demands, its institutional identity – and spiritual transformation. To get close to an artist like El Greco, Sherrard suggests, it may be necessary

> to burrow beneath our western Christian heritage. ... We have to get behind our Puritanism, behind our preoccupation with ethics, behind our feeling that the supernatural world, if it exists at all, is something static, passionless, free from inner desire. We have to get beyond our feeling that life is an expiation for some terrible sin and that God is a tribunal.[24]

In the West God has been made 'an intellectual principle or a moral code';[25] and that has had severe consequences. In worshipping a 'passionless God', one 'free from desire', the West has been guilty of 'murdering our own humanity and that of the world', particularly in the denial of the erotic that has characterised Western Christianity, Catholic and Protestant alike. Consequently, as Sherrard puts it, 'we have murdered the humanity of our God. And in so doing we have deprived both the world and this God of ours of life. We have turned both [God and our humanity] into something impersonal, outside ourselves, scientific objects.'[26]

This objectification has, Sherrard admits, made certain things possible, among them modern science: we can 'dissect the world'. And with God now an abstraction, we can 'speculate on the nature of God ... whether he is pure idea, or limitless will, or just an illusion'. But 'in the end it has killed off our God altogether ... God: what an empty, meaningless word, quite dead on the tongue, with the taste of ashes.'[27]

---

24. *Blood and Light*, p. 185.
25. Ibid.
26. Ibid.
27. Ibid.

III

That anger against the Western God is the context for Sherrard's approach, in the first years of the 1950s, to the orthodoxy he adopted in 1956. Between 1950 and 1952 Sherrard was able to return to Greece for an extended period, through his connection with the British School of Archaeology in Athens, of which he became assistant director in 1951. It was during that time that he met George Seferis in person for the first time.[28] Then, in April 1951, he spent two weeks at the centre of orthodox monasticism, Mount Athos; and in the same month he gave a lecture on St Symeon at the British School. At the same time, he was developing his knowledge of the Greek Fathers.[29]

Among those, St Symeon had particular importance for Sherrard; like him, he was a theologian and poet. Born in Asia Minor in the mid-tenth century, he was the abbot of the monastery of St Mamas, and he left a rich body of poetry and sermons. He was versed in the long tradition of the Greek Fathers, among them Gregory of Nyssa and Maximus the Confessor. Because he came some centuries after them he was called 'the Young' and 'the New Theologian'. For Sherrard, he voiced that long tradition.

Sherrard's religious position in his earlier life, if he had one, is not clear from the published material. The early poetry, riddled with despair, carries no trace of any faith, least of all anything specifically Christian. In his early essays and lectures, critical though he is of the faith of others, he does not speak of any faith of his own. The circumstances of his childhood and youth – his mother's rejection of convention, the free-thinking ambience of Bloomsbury – do not suggest an engagement with any of the forms of Christianity that might have been available. His brief experience of public school and his two years at Cambridge probably did little to change that.

---

28. On 29 December 1950 (*Blood and Light*, p. 167).
29. *Blood and Light*, p. 167.

Nothing suggests that Sherrard's move to orthodoxy was a conversion from public school Anglicanism to an aesthetically more appealing faith; rather it was a philosophical step he felt obliged to take. In his letter to Seferis of 6 January 1949, he had spoken of seeing the world 'simply as a destructive mechanical process' and of 'having no other pole towards which to turn'.[30] There had to be an opening towards a larger 'other'; as he says in the El Greco lecture of 1950, humanity requires a 'sense of reciprocity'; there is 'this Other, who is the determining principle of man's personality and of his humanity'.[31] Without knowledge of that 'other', humanity cannot sustain itself; it requires an interlocutor simply to remain human.

It was for that reason that Sherrard, Platonist though he was in many respects, could not in the end settle to the Platonic world of pure transcendental ideas. He makes clear its inadequacy at the start of his lecture on St Symeon. Such a world was in essence impersonal, 'a world of ideas, an impersonal *kosmos noetos*', a reality that existed only in thought. The Platonic intellect, seeking understanding,

> in its search for an ideal world could not recognize anything which was unlike itself, [and so] when it considered man it could only recognize in man what was capable of rationalization, the idea of man, in fact an abstract man. This side of man is, in the same way as the Platonic world of Ideas, something essentially impersonal. The personal side of man is too complex, too contradictory, too irrational for the mind to grasp.[32]

To be a person, for Sherrard, was to exist within that complexity; personhood, for him, was in intimate relation to what lay beyond reason. Platonism tended toward a dismissal of all that. But it also

---

30. *Blood and Light*, p. 81.
31. *Blood and Light*, p. 187.
32. *Blood and Light*, pp. 198–9.

proposed a universe in which personhood was not required; where the ideas, in their eternal impersonality, were alone ultimately real.

He begins with a general statement about the history of the Western mind – that the origin of its rationalism is to be found in ancient Greece. The post-Socratic thinkers took the view 'that it is possible to reach an understanding of reality by means of the intellect alone; that it is possible to ascertain truth by asking rational questions and by giving rational answers'.[33] Only reason that could recognise had reality. Those aspects of humanity that resisted incorporation by reason were therefore seen as lacking reality, and the rational life of the intellect became the criterion of what it was to be human. From that grew the ideal of the rational man, the 'abstract man' from whom the complexities of irrationality were to be discarded.

The result was a constriction of vision, the exclusion of much that is human. Against that reduction, Sherrard argues that it was Christianity's 'great effort' to restore a wider vision by placing the person in all its complexity at the centre. This was not a purely ethical matter, an insistence on the value of each individual; it was also an expansion of what might be known, a personalisation of the idea of truth. 'Truth for the Christians was not an object which could be known by the intellect alone. It was not an object at all. It was a subject, in fact a person. ... Truth was a person who could love and hate, who could sorrow and rejoice.'[34] Clearly and decisively for the rest of his thinking, and as early as 1951, Sherrard rejects the objectification of the person. The guarantee of that was the figure of Christ, personhood at the centre of being.

A personal truth, a truth that grows from personhood, changes the one who knows. Whereas an external, factual, objective truth can be known without any change in the knower, a personal truth

---

33. *Blood and Light*, p. 198.
34. *Blood and Light*, p. 199.

must, Sherrard believes, transform. Christianity was therefore necessarily transfiguration, not intellectual definition and statement, least of all subordination to a corporate institution. And the entry to that transformation was not an argument but initiation. For the first time Sherrard draws a parallel between Christianity and the ancient Mystery religions. Speaking of the roots of Christianity, he says that 'the language of the Christians was much more like that of the pagan mystery religions than that of the philosophers'; religions that

offered to those who partook of [the mysteries] an experience of an intense nature which transcended the limits of this world and gave the assurance of personal salvation. At the base of all mysticism is the belief that in the depths of the human soul the mortal and the immortal worlds touch.[35]

Christianity emerged as just such a mysticism, a conjunction of the two worlds. Prefiguring what he will later say about the Eucharist, Sherrard sees the initiates of the mystery religions as entering into a 'mystic drama, a divine progress which was the principle and prototype of salvation'. This was also true of early Christianity. The point of Christianity 'was not [to] build an ideal philosophical system or even carry out good works'; the knowledge it had to offer came not from concept but from that mystical point of contact between 'the mortal and the immortal worlds'.

This combination of initiation and transformation is at the heart of Sherrard's understanding of Christianity. The transformation is not primarily moral; it is of the whole being, physical as well as ethical and intellectual. Already in the El Greco lecture he had excoriated Western Christianity for its rejection of the body; now in this Byzantine theologian he finds a Christianity that can speak in

---

35. *Blood and Light*, p. 200.

bodily, even erotic, terms. He quotes St Symeon: 'and we shall become as Gods, joined in intimacy to God, showing no stain on our body but all being in likeness to the whole body of Christ, each one of us having as our limbs the complete Christ.'[36]

To speak of 'the body of Christ' opens the matter of Incarnation; and Sherrard's critique of the West continues. There 'the' Incarnation has been understood almost wholly in historical terms, as a unique event that happened at a precise moment, in the life of one man. But for St Symeon and the Byzantine tradition the Incarnation and the Resurrection 'were not only things which had happened once, in the past. They were things which were entirely present and should happen to every man.'[37] For them, the Incarnation revealed what is true of all humanity: each human being is a unity of the physical and the divine. It tells us who we are.

Such an understanding transforms what it is to be human. The question that Sherrard must address, though, is how such things can be known. He has already rejected the idea that existential truth can be a matter of pure intellect, the conclusion of a rational argument. He is now ready to claim that such truth is known in an immediate way; it is a matter of vision, perceived rather than analytically established. There is a moment when, before its translation into concept, truth presents itself preconceptually and is recognised. These recognitions are, for Sherrard, mystical and veridical. It is knowing of that kind that he finds in St Symeon, who 'to the affective mysticism of eros ... unites the speculative mysticism of "gnosis"'.[38]

It is not immediately clear what kind of 'gnosis', or knowledge, Sherrard has in mind. He was not a gnostic. He did not believe that salvation lay in occult wisdom. He did not reject materiality as evil; rather, he insisted on the goodness of all being. In his later writing

---

36. St Symeon, *Ethical Discourses* I, 1. Quoted in *Blood and Light*, p. 203.
37. *Blood and Light*, p. 205.
38. *Blood and Light*, p. 207.

he explicitly rejects Gnosticism.[39] Yet he does speak of 'gnosis' (uncapitalised), and often suggests that we have some faculty, some capacity for direct knowledge, that uniquely allows us to know spiritual truths.

How, then, is this word to be understood? Sherrard's focus is on knowledge not derived from concept. Just as Seferis and El Greco knew their worlds through the substance of their art, image or symbol or paint, and so conveyed a knowledge not mediated through concept, so that which the mystic knows is also before and beyond concept. His 'gnosis' is the moment of first encounter, when meaning is simply the thing itself: a face, a mountain, a chord of music, recognition not interpretation, a matter of experience, of the senses even, not of ideas. For Sherrard all spiritual truth is known in that way. Just as Incarnation is not a unique event but the state of being human, so 'gnosis' is nothing remote or special: it is simply the way that human beings recognise transformative truth.

'Gnosis' carries for Sherrard the possibility of an inclusive vision, a way of seeing in which the elements of human knowing, sensory as well as intellectual, come together in a single act. Seferis had shown him that. Here he turns again to poetry, this time the poetry of St Symeon. After the trauma of war and the desolate years that followed, he was ready, however tentatively, to borrow the words of this Byzantine saint. Perhaps there was a total knowledge that was also the knowledge of God:

Solitary, one who is unmixed with the world,
and continually speaks with God alone.

---

39. This is clearest in his essay 'Forms of Sacred Cosmology in the Pre-Renaissance World', the first chapter of *Human Image: World Image* (Ipswich: Golgonooza Press, 1992; reprinted Limni, Evia, Greece: Denise Harvey (Publisher), 2004). On page 17 he speaks with disapproval of the gnostics as 'positing a totally disembodied, extraterrestrial, pure God, removed as far as possible from all contact with or regard for the world.'

Seeing, he is seen, loving he is loved,
and becomes light glittering unspeakably.[40]

IV

Throughout the late 1940s and early 1950s Sherrard was deepening his engagement with Greek culture. The letters to Seferis are a record of that, of his work of translation and his immersion in Greek poetry that went beyond Seferis to include others, particularly Angelos Sikelianos and Constantine P. Cavafy.[41] Though his first volume of translations did not appear until several years later,[42] he was already publishing translations in journals.[43]

This broader interest in Greek poetry began to take shape when, in 1949, he gained a Spalding Fellowship at King's College, London, to work toward a PhD. The proposed subject was Greek poetry. Because of time spent in Greece during the following years, this work was in suspense until September 1952. By 1954, though, he was ready to submit his dissertation, entitled 'Three Modern Greek Poets: A Critical Survey'.

The three poets were Dionysios Solomos, Gregory Palamas and Seferis. In the next two years (the doctorate was awarded in 1956) he revised and expanded his dissertation, and in the same year it was published as *The Marble Threshing Floor*.[44] Apart from his poetry

---

40. St Symeon, *Hymn 3*. Quoted in *Blood and Light* 208.
41. He was translating Cavafy as early as November 1948 (*Blood and Light*, p. 75).
42. *Six Poets of Modern Greece* (with Edmund Keeley) (London: Thames and Hudson, 1960).
43. The correspondence with Seferis includes many references to John Lehmann and *New Writing*, but it is not clear from that record that Sherrard ever succeeded in placing translations with him.
44. Philip Sherrard, *The Marble Threshing Floor: Studies in Modern Greek Poetry* (London: Vallentine Mitchell, 1956; reprinted Limni, Evia, Greece: Denise Harvey (Publisher), 1981 and 1992). Referred to subsequently as *Marble Threshing*. The main work for the book seems

collection *Orientation and Descent* in 1953, this was Sherrard's first book. To the three poets of the dissertation, he added Constantine Cavafy and Angelos Sikelianos.

The Marble Threshing Floor was the first English-language study to deal extensively and in depth with modern Greek poetry as it emerged in the nineteenth and twentieth centuries. It bears some marks of its origin as a thesis. In a workmanlike survey of its field, giving due attention to each of the poets, there is a tendency to overload the text with paraphrase. But it is more than an impersonal academic study: it is clearly directed by Sherrard's own concerns.

This emerges in his choice of poets and in his commentary. A main criterion for his evaluation of these poets is the extent to which they connect with that 'other world' that was so important to him in his 1948 discussion of Seferis. He says of Solomos that the poet's heroic characters appear 'to achieve a certain release by contact with some invisible power', and Solomos himself, he suggests, felt 'a growing conviction that man's true life was not to be realised in this world, but in the attainment of a level of reality of which this world was the negation'.[45] Again as with Seferis in 1948, tradition is seen as a way of knowing. The strength of Solomos's poetry is ascribed, at least in part, to 'principles enshrined and preserved in a living religious tradition', and many of his ideas 'come, if not from the dawn of history, at least from an early age ... [ideas] implicit in the art forms of many cultures'.[46] In Solomos Sherrard finds a way of knowing akin to his own 'gnosis'; and he speaks of contemplation. All art begins

> with a supra-individual world that cannot be known by observation or discursive reasoning but only by contem-

---

to have been done in 1954 and 1955: the final chapter is dated 'Highgate, 1954' and the Preface 'Athens, November, 1955'.

45. *Marble Threshing*, p. 14.
46. *Marble Threshing*, p. 17.

plation. This is the world of spiritual realities, of archetypes and of archetypal experience, and it is the task of the artist to embody this world in his work. The artistic process begins, then, with the artist's intuition of this world.[47]

The language is Platonic; but the vital point for Sherrard is that the poet is one who knows, but knows with a directness beyond that of concept and rationalisation.

Once again Sherrard is looking to expand the bounds of the knowable. On that depends the possibility of an integrated humanity, not riven by opposition between mind and body, matter and spirit. Solomos, he says, fails in that respect. He 'recognises a duality in life, a duality in reality ... the world of the spirit, which is good, and the world of the flesh, which is evil';[48] but the duality remains unresolved, a dualism of opposites. In Palamas he sees a 'division in his soul, product of his dualistic attitude to life, his sense of life's present horror' against 'a once-known world of beauty and harmony'.[49] In Cavafy the dualism is that of an aesthetic mode of being set against the world of 'time and death'. Cavafy cannot resolve that opposition; as the body declines, his only refuge is aesthetic irony, beauty made ironic by decay.

The poet who joins the three of the doctorates, and the one given the longest chapter, is Angelos Sikelianos; this is partly because Sherrard sees him as coming closest to resolving this problem of dualism. In Sikelianos there is a myth of primal unity:

All in the beginning was part of one whole, of a primordial unity. ... On the one hand, all natural forms are the manifestation of an original divine life, and are therefore holy. On the

---

47. *Marble Threshing*, p. 19.
48. *Marble Threshing*, p. 37.
49. *Marble Threshing*, p. 51.

other hand, these same forms witness to the dismemberment of this original life. ... Through the attainment of spiritual vision, which is the realisation of his own nature, [man] brings together the worlds which have fallen apart, he restores their original unity.[50]

In Sikelianos Sherrard found an echo of his own struggle, between a fragmented reality and the search for a unifying vision. If to overcome what had 'fallen apart' was Sikelianos's aspiration, it was equally Sherrard's. Speaking as much for himself as for Sikelianos, Sherrard sees that vision as the fruit of contemplation; and in that the modern West has failed:

Ages which are creative ... are those in which the human mind keeps, through contemplation, its contacts with the ideas, or forms, of an Intelligence which is itself beyond the mind's natural reason. To exalt the reason at the expense of this Intelligence to the extent to which the West has done, is to invite destruction.[51]

V

In the fifth chapter of *The Marble Threshing Floor* Sherrard turns again to George Seferis, almost a decade after his first discussion of the poet in 1948. For Sherrard, Seferis's great strength remains what it had been: the power, through symbolic language, to unite medium and meaning, and so to point beyond contemporary confusion to a deeper source. The confusions of 1956 are no less than those of 1948: 'all round man in the contemporary world is a chaos of forces and events which seem on the surface to be utterly unrelated, unregulated, impersonal and pointless.' Sherrard speaks of 'the black

---

50. *Marble Threshing*, p. 127.
51. *Marble Threshing*, p. 174.

world of phenomena', 'the great chaotic flux of things'.[52] Against that, Seferis senses another reality, dormant and perhaps out of reach, but present still in its very absence – not an intellectual solution but a response to the materiality of the world. Sherrard quotes Seferis's 'Letter on the "*Thrush*"': 'my task is not with abstract ideas but to hear what the things of the world say to me, to discern how they interweave themselves with my soul and body, and to express them.'[53]

As with Sikelianos, such discernment has its root in contemplation. Sherrard sees Seferis as representative of those artists whose orientation is toward 'a still centre of contemplative understanding', and he points to the 1932 poem '*The Cistern*'. There silent engagement with the being of the world is richly present. Sherrard quotes the first line, 'Here, in the earth, is a cistern rooted', and continues:

It is rooted in the earth. It gathers only secret water. Outside and above it, the vast tumultuous life of the world goes on. ... But the cistern remains untouched, a still heart in the centre of life, a source which gathers to itself the pains and struggles of the outside world. ... This cistern, this still heart, is, then, the image of some presence which lies within us; it is in some sense our most intimate being.[54]

This presence has 'the nature of an obscure, unmanifested intelligence which is at the root of life. It is a kind of understanding without action.'[55] Seferis's vision is single: object and meaning,

---

52. *Marble Threshing*, p 186.
53. George Seferis, 'A Letter on the "*Thrush*"', *Anglo–Greek Review*, 4 (12), July–August 1950, p. 504. The 'Letter' is reprinted in George Seferis, *On the Greek Style* (London: The Bodley Head, 1966), pp. 107–17. This passage quoted in *Marble Threshing*, p. 186.
54. *Marble Threshing*, p. 187–8.
55. *Marble Threshing*, p. 193.

symbol and referent, are inseparable. The world does not need to be translated; the cistern *is* what it means.

If Sherrard's response to this poetry involves a withdrawal from concept, it also involves a rejection of Western individualism, of the individual as the normative human ideal. In Seferis's long poem 'Mythistorema' (1933) Sherrard sees 'a journey to the dead', imaged by the journey of the Argonauts. But that is more than a device, a literary trope. Just as Plato had said that being a philosopher was a study of dying, so, for Sherrard, the path to understanding, to 'gnosis', lies in the loss of the external trappings of individuality, a dying to the selfhood that we habitually cultivate:

> What is signified by such dying and death is a process of detachment from the false, superficial selfhood, that which makes the eyes and ears bad witnesses, in order to recover possession of the deeper self when all can be seen in its proper light. It is as if man, looking in a mirror, mistook the image of himself in it for his real self, a kind of Narcissus intoxication.[56]

Sherrard quotes Blake: 'Each Man is in his Spectre's power'.

Seferis reaches for this original selfhood in his effort to recover the King of Asine. Seferis's poem of 1940 grows from the slightest passing reference in Homer. In the Iliad, in the catalogue of ships, the king is mentioned almost as an afterthought: 'Asinin te.'[57] We learn nothing about him. He is an absence, undefined, without feature; yet tangible, always present:

> The King of Asine, whom we seek for two years now
> unknown, forgotten by everyone, even by Homer

---

56. *Marble Threshing*, p. 218.
57. Iliad, ii, 560. Listing the sources of the ships that sailed to Troy, the full line translates: 'From Argos, and Tiryns of the great walls, from Hermione and Asine.'

only one word in the Iliad, and that uncertain
flung here like a gold funeral mask ...
The King of Asine an emptiness under the mask
Everywhere with us everywhere with us, under one name:
'Asinin te ... Asinin te.'[58]

Though Sherrard responds to Seferis's evocation of the hidden, of silent presence, he finds there a danger: such quietism may drift into fatalism. In a qualification not there in the 1948 essay, he speaks of 'a certain failure of nerve'[59] in Seferis's approach to life. The 'Odyssey' is at the centre of his imaginative world; from it, Sherrard suspects, Seferis has drawn the idea of fate overruling all human purposes, placing human existence in the hands of an impersonal force.

That unease with fatalism may cast some light on a moment of difficulty in their correspondence. In March 1956 Sherrard, in Athens, wrote to Seferis:

> I came back from London a few days ago and found your poems here. ... The truth is that I get increasingly bigoted about poetry, and demand more and more from it that it should represent and serve [the great essences][60] and where it doesn't I am disappointed.[61]

This was partly in response to some words of Seferis, in a letter of the previous year, saying that he was in no sense a metaphysician. If he had a metaphysics, it came from immediate experience:

---

58. George Seferis, 'The King of Asine', in *Logbook I* (Athens, 1940). Sherrard's 1956 translation in *Marble Threshing*, p. 220.
59. *Marble Threshing*, p. 206.
60. A phrase from Sikelianos; in Greek in the original, translated in *Blood and Light*.
61. *Blood and Light*, p. 271.

An old woman dandling her great-grandchild, an old Druse who was angry because people were eating the mulberries off his mulberry tree – the only tree he possessed – a little village girl in Cyprus who danced like a princess. I have never been a philosopher or a metaphysician – my metaphysics (for the metaphysicians) arise out of my attachment to such things – if it exists at all – and if it doesn't, well, I am a poor man.[62]

Paradoxically, there is much here that is close to Sherrard: the immediacy of the world, the rejection of abstraction. But Sherrard also felt the need for some metaphysical superstructure, some 'other world' that might contain that immediate vision. In his reply of April 1956 Seferis pursues the point, again using the phrase from Sikelianos. He has, he says, often found 'the great essences' to ring hollow.[63]

Seferis was suspicious of 'the great essences'; for Sherrard they were a necessary dimension, the 'other world' that was at the heart of the artist's vocation. For a while their correspondence seems to have cooled. Despite his desire to avoid abstraction and intellectualisation, at this moment Sherrard is more the metaphysician, and it is Seferis who holds to the immediate. Sherrard's demand for poetry to deliver 'the great essences' shows him looking for a framework for his thought. It was in the same year that he was received into the Orthodox Church.

VI

Though the subject of *The Marble Threshing Floor* is modern Greek poetry, in its course Sherrard's ideas emerge more and more clearly.

---

62. George Seferis, draft letter in Greek to Philip Sherrard of July 1955, translated in *Blood and Light*, 268–70.
63. George Seferis, letter to Philip Sherrard of 6 April 1956 (*Blood and Light*, p. 272).

The final chapter, 'The Poetry and the Myth', is a summation of where his discussions had led him. His position is explicitly Platonic. Art begins, not in imitation of the world, but 'in a super-sensual world whose forms the artist has come to understand'.[64] These supersensual forms, which he calls archetypes, are known not by reasoning but by contemplation. In language that moves towards Orthodoxy, these forms are rooted in a 'universal Wisdom', knowledge of which is the wisdom of the artist. This sets Sherrard, as he well realises, against what he calls 'the "humanist" culture of the last few centuries',[65] against a West that prioritises individualism and individuality of style, that sees art as a vehicle for personal self-expression, not as grounded in the 'abyss of history', in the common mind of tradition. Greece, he claims, has escaped that shift; the Byzantine centuries sustained a tradition embodied in 'the Christian myth' but reaching back to the ancient world, to the myths of the Orphic and Pythagorean mysteries. Having lost the fullness of such an inheritance, the culture of the West has narrowed, into a rationalist truth and an ethical religion. With that radical dualisms have appeared: of good and evil, of fact and meaning, of body and mind. The result has been a humanity caught more and more in the crossfire of irreconcilables.

Sherrard is aware that in stating the problem as he often does – the 'sensible' world set against the 'supersensual' – he risks opening a deeper dualism between two modes of being. In this final chapter he confronts that danger:

> We must be careful not to assume that when poets like Solomos ... posit or imply the existence of a level of reality other than that which can be seen and touched, they neces-sarily mean that there is another world existing alongside or

---

64. *Marble Threshing*, p. 233.
65. *Marble Threshing*, p. 234.

parallel to this visible, tangible world, one that is just as 'objective' and 'factual' as this world, only in another dimension.[66]

Though it may be 'impossible to *think* of the temporal and the eternal worlds except as two distinct worlds', that must be resisted; and there is a weapon against such dualism of thought, which is myth. Myth, free from obligation to concept, is able 'to reveal to us the actual participation of the temporal in the eternal', the 'simultaneity' of the two realities 'not in terms of objective facts, but in terms of actual experience'.[67] It is there, at that point of simultaneity, that humanly defining truth is to be found.

Here another of Sherrard's central themes can be seen emerging, that of participation. The temporal and the eternal participate in each other; true vision sees that participation rejects a rationalisation that sets them apart. It is the struggle towards that vision that Sherrard finds most compelling in Greek poetry. But the dualisms of his world remain; and in his next book he traces their sources, looks to see what it is that has brought the Western world to the disjunctions and alienations that, from his perspective in Greece, he can see only too clearly.

---

66. *Marble Threshing*, p. 244.
67. Ibid.

2

Reason and the West

Philip Sherrard's second book, *The Greek East and the Latin West*, was published in 1959.[1] In 1957 he had begun a fellowship at St Antony's College, Oxford, but in 1958 he was offered the position of assistant director of the British School of Archaeology in Athens. This allowed him to return to Greece; and it was the stimulus of that return and release from a formal academic setting that energised his completion of this complex book. He held the post in Athens until 1961, and during those years he published a great deal. Besides *The Greek East and the Latin West*, there was his book on Athos[2] and his first collection of translations from Greek poetry.[3] But it is *The Greek East and the Latin West* that is central to those years and, intellectually, to the rest of his writing career.

The book could hardly have been predicted from Sherrard's earlier writing. Aside from his poetry, he had written short essays on specific topics (such as St Symeon and El Greco) and one extended piece of literary criticism, *The Marble Threshing Floor*. The new

---

1. Philip Sherrard, *The Greek East and the Latin West* (London: Oxford University Press, 1959; reissued with a new Appendix, Limni, Evia, Greece: Denise Harvey (Publisher), 1992 and 1995). Referred to subsequently as *Greek East and Latin West*.
2. Philip Sherrard, *Athos: The Mountain of Silence* (London: Oxford University Press, 1960).
3. *Six Poets of Modern Greece*. Translated and Introduced by Edmund Keeley and Philip Sherrard. (London: Thames and Hudson, 1960).

book was a long theologico-philosophical argument, drawing on his reading of Greek philosophy and the Greek Fathers. In it he seeks to find the origins of those deficiencies of Western culture that he had identified but not accounted for in his earlier writing. In it, the question of a unifying vision is addressed in philosophical terms. What earlier had been approached through the language of poetry or the power of paint on a canvas is now addressed through the record of an intellectual descent, one that begins with Aristotle and shapes the parameters of the Western mind down to the present.

This descent takes the form of a fracturing of the ways of knowing, a disjunction, intensifying across the centuries, between the cognitive resources that Sherrard gathers under the word 'gnosis' – myth, tradition, symbol, the immediacy of the preconceptual world – and reason. He finds a progressive incapacity in the Western mind for any whole vision. As the West moves further into concept and distinction, as it sees measurement and quantification as the tools of real knowledge, so the knowledge that is made real in a Seferis or an El Greco moves to the margins of human awareness.

The title of the book suggests the argument: a comparison of the Greek Christianity of the East and the Latin Christianity of the West, of how each understands the nature of God; but there are also different understandings of what it is to be human and different definitions of the knowable. For Sherrard, the decisive point was the Western rediscovery of Aristotle in the thirteenth century. In Aquinas and the scholastics, the West committed itself to a specific epistemology, a dualism of revelation and reason. Out of that grew modern science; but out of it too grew an inability to sustain a unitary vision, one that might include, with the facts of the material world, the spiritual experience of humanity.

I

That moment in the thirteenth century had, nevertheless, a long history. Sherrard traces it back to Greek philosophy, to Plato and

Aristotle; and the contrast between them is the foundation of the argument of this book.

Much of the argument of this book revolves around the classical concept of form, that immaterial reality that gives identity to existing things: makes them good or beautiful or just what they are, a horse or a tree. Forms may be understood as universals: their reality may be thought of as independent of the particular objects in which they present themselves. How this concept is used is central to Sherrard's distinction between Plato and Aristotle.

Sherrard begins with Plato and suggests 'that Plato himself stood at the end, rather than at the beginning, of a tradition of religious thought'.[4] Before Plato there had been a tradition, one that did not express itself in philosophical terms because such terms were inadequate; essentially mystical, it was grounded in experience that could not be reduced to the rationality of language (Sherrard refers to Pythagoras and the mystery cults). Plato's effort was to express that tradition in philosophical terms, but that already involved a loss: 'there is already implicit in the method of Plato a danger that the very ideas he sought to express will be falsified.'[5]

Yet much survives in Plato, and that is what draws Sherrard to him. Human vision should include that which transcends it, the 'other world' of his discussion of Seferis. Sherrard requires a supernatural reality, and that he finds in Plato. On the one hand there is the world available to the senses and on the other the ideas, the archetypes: 'in the Platonic view, sensible existence is the outcome of the interaction between the principle of form and formless matter.'[6] For Plato 'these Ideas, or principial forms, have an objective reality of their own, quite independent both of their corresponding sensible objects and of the mind of any individual thinking subject'.[7] In Plato's thinking

---

4. *Greek East and Latin West*, p. 5.
5. Ibid.
6. *Greek East and Latin West*, p. 6.
7. *Greek East and Latin West*, pp. 6–7.

supernature is real; the natural, the material, the transient depend on that which transcends them. Sherrard's requirement is satisfied.

Aristotle, on the other hand, falls short. Though for him too form is central to his thinking, it functions quite differently. He does not allow the forms any existence independent of their material instantiations: 'Aristotle was unable to visualize the existence of such forms apart from their sensible objects.'[8] Forms do not constitute a reality that transcends the world of matter. The reality of the forms for Aristotle is essentially conceptual: they are universals (of quality, of geometrical structure) that the mind generates from the observation of particulars. They are not unreal, but they possess only the reality that belongs to universals.

Sherrard's thinking tends generally toward Platonism, and the roots of that can be seen in this contrast. Yet, if the Platonic view better sustains a transcendental reality, there are still problems, and they derive from Sherrard's opposition to dualism. Here he finds himself in some difficulty with Plato. He suspects that the Platonic model of being, with its distinction between the eternal forms and sensible reality, may constitute a dualism. By contrast, the Aristotelian model, where the forms are immanent within material objects, may escape such a charge. For Aristotle there is only one thing: form-and-matter, inseparable, a single mode of being.

Sherrard argues that Plato overcomes this difficulty by placing the form-matter duality within a larger unity. Plato placed his supreme reality, the Good, beyond both the forms and material reality, the world of the senses: 'the principle of form ... is not the supreme reality, the Good; it is a determination of [determined by] the Good, while the Good itself transcends all formal characteristics.'[9] Nor does Aristotle's 'First Mover' offer what Sherrard is looking for; it is in essence a logical construct required by the fact

---

8.   *Greek East and Latin West*, p. 7.
9.   *Greek East and Latin West*, p. 6.

of change within material entities. 'It is neither the pre-formal and undetermined reality of which the principle of cosmic form, and the creative Ideas, are themselves determinations, nor is it really even the creative principle of actual sensible objects.'[10] Compared with Plato's Good it is a verbal nullity, certainly inadequate to be the 'other' in which all being is contained. At the level of the Good there is, for Plato, no duality and so no risk of dualism.

This question, of a possible dualism in Plato's thinking, is one that Sherrard returns to more than once.[11] For the moment, an answer has been suggested. But Sherrard's real problem lies with the idea of a supernature, however described. Such an idea seems necessarily to imply a dualism vis-à-vis nature. Whether the supernature is called the Good or God, it is hard for it not to stand over against material reality and human existence itself.

Sherrard struggles with that problem across the years. But if dualisms trouble him, so does monism; and it is a version of monism that he fears in Aristotle. Yes, Aristotle avoids the potential dualism of form and matter: they are not to be separated, can never appear apart. But the price is the exclusion of the 'other', that dimension that Sherrard finds essential for any whole vision of reality. Form, the 'other', is dissolved into the materiality of entities. Sherrard opposes dualisms but not dualities; in a duality, of form and matter, of body and spirit, neither element is dissolved into the other. Both retain their reality in a mutuality of participation. Sherrard suspects Aristotle of collapsing a real duality into a false monism; a move that he sees perpetuated in the scientific mind of the West.

Sherrard has further difficulties with Aristotle. One of the implications for Sherrard of Aristotle's general position is a limitation on what may be known:

---

10. *Greek East and Latin West*, p. 7.
11. For example, in the first chapter of *Human Image: World Image* (1992), and in his late essay 'The Challenge of Plethon and Nietzsche', in *Christianity: Lineaments of a Sacred Tradition* (1998).

Once ... it was denied that the creative forms of things, their divine Ideas, have any objective reality apart from their existence in sensible objects or in the individual mind of a thinking subject, the type of spiritual realization envisaged by Plato, and the mode of knowledge proper to it, is, of course, impossible. Man cannot intuit the divine and supernatural realities apart from their corporeal forms if they are not there to be intuited.[12]

What is left within the Aristotelian frame is rational knowledge, knowledge limited to the operation of reason. Even the forms themselves, deduced from observation of the sensible world, are the product of reason and as such abstractions: 'the supreme arbiter of form is the reason, what constitutes form being such rational and logical characteristics as the reason can discern and conceptualize.'[13]

Against Aristotle, Sherrard wishes to preserve the human capacity that earlier he called 'gnosis'. The contrast with Plato is once more relevant. Within the Platonic scheme, there is a mode of knowing that is not primarily that of reason: the knowing of *anamnesis*, of recollection. Sherrard's 'gnosis' comes close to that. It is itself recognition, of what is already known at a level prior to that of the reason: recognition of the good and the beautiful, neither of which is the fruit of any deduction. Sherrard is prepared to extend that to all spiritual truth. We have the capacity to recognise it; we do not argue ourselves into it.

II

There is for Sherrard a narrowing Aristotelian inheritance in the Western mind; and he goes on to look at its consequences for

---

12. *Greek East and Latin West*, p. 8–9.
13. *Greek East and Latin West*, p. 9.

Christianity in the late classical world. In the first chapter of *The Greek East and the Latin West*, writing of the 'Roman Background', he describes how the priority given to reason in Aristotelian thought produced a suspicion, not to say a fear, of whatever was perceived as irrational. Since reason was the measure of the knowable, the irrational stood outside what might properly be known, and was therefore lacking reality; within the Aristotelian frame 'the more rationality an object possesses, the greater its degree of reality, and hence its value, and this whether the object in question is an institution, a work of art, or the conduct of a human life; and, of course, the converse is true as well.'[14]

A consequence was the marginalisation of the pre-Socratic mystery traditions. Roman public religion founded itself on the rational organisation of human affairs:

> The Divine came to be regarded as a static and abstract order, essentially rational in its nature … it followed that what was formless, in movement, and irrational was felt to a corresponding degree to lack divine qualities; it was felt to lack reality and even to be entirely negative and evil.[15]

Out of that came what Sherrard characterises as a 'Ciceronian' public ideology. For Cicero, 'it is the reason alone which is capable of realizing that knowledge [of the civilised life] by revealing the "divine" order of nature, the law of which is identical with that of "right reason".' It is reason that is 'the link between man and man, and man and God'.[16] In such a setting religion itself becomes suspect: as 'unreason', it is seen as superstition, and the gods as illusory beings created by the human mind. Sherrard sees a line of connection from this rationalistic cult to the later humanisms of Europe.

---

14. *Greek East and Latin West*, p. 9.
15. *Greek East and Latin West*, p. 11.
16. *Greek East and Latin West*, p. 15.

Into that Roman world Christianity entered; and with Constantine's conversion in the fourth century, it came to hold sway over it. In describing that transition Sherrard begins from the Christianity of the pre-Constantinian period. His characterisation of early Christianity is a personal one and it remains with him through most of his writing. It does not, for example, make much of the position of Jesus; across his writing, that name is hardly ever used. Instead, Sherrard describes the faith in more general terms:

> To give an outline of the Christian doctrine, two things must be said. ... The first is that what must always be borne in mind when speaking of the Christian doctrine is that Christianity is above all a Way, 'the Way of God' or 'Way of salvation', and not a philosophy or a system of human thought.[17]

As such, it stood in opposition to the rational humanism of the Ciceronian kind. But Sherrard's interpretation also universalises Christianity; it becomes a spiritual path among paths, not defined by historical events. Indeed, Sherrard goes on to qualify the idea that Christianity is a historical religion at all. Here he departs from much contemporary theological thought. The assertion of the historical nature of the faith has been a frequent trope in modern Christian apologetics: Christianity is worth attention because it is not just 'spiritual' but grounded in fact. Sherrard takes the point: Christianity, like Judaism and unlike Platonism, takes history seriously, as 'the epiphany of God, the scene of action of a divine-human drama of cosmic significance'.[18] But the historical emphasis has had undesirable consequences:

> So great in fact has been the value given to historical events and personages that not only has their essentially relative

---

17. *Greek East and Latin West*, p. 27.
18. *Greek East and Latin West*, p. 30.

nature when compared with the 'eternal now' of the extra-temporal world been obscured; but it has even been forgotten altogether that Christianity possesses a genuinely meta-physical, and therefore non-historical side.[19]

At such points it is possible to detect in Sherrard an inclination towards the *philosophia perennis*: Christianity is one way, but it stands parallel to other and less historical cults.

This qualified de-historicisation of Christianity has implica-tions for Sherrard's understanding of its main tenets. As he argued in his 1951 discussion of St Symeon, the Incarnation and the Resurrection are less unique historical events, more revelations of what has always and everywhere been the case: that the human embodies the divine and so is not cancelled by death. He takes a word from St John's gospel:

> The Incarnation and the Resurrection are not … only 'facts' of one particular historical period and place which once and for all liberated mankind and the world from the power of the 'prince of this world'. On the contrary, they are as it were continuing operations of the Logos in which mankind should consciously participate through all time.[20]

Participation is the vital point: true human identity is to be found in participation in the Logos, in God as realised in the created world. But most directly this operation of the Logos is to be found 'in the Mysteries which He [the Logos] initiates', and the place of those mysteries is the Church. Once again Sherrard's language recalls the ancient mystery religions: 'these Mysteries, and the mystagogical life which centres round them, constitute, in their totality, the Church.'[21]

---

19. Ibid.
20. *Greek East and Latin West*, p. 44.
21. *Greek East and Latin West*, p. 45.

It is that mystery-based characterisation of the Church that gives Sherrard's account of Christianity its particular emphasis. The Church is the place of mysteries, which he equates with the sacraments; and as mysteries they are transformative for those who partake in them. As a place of mysteries, the Church is entered through initiation, but Sherrard does not mention baptism. The Eucharist is the entrance to the mystery. The 'aspirant' is initiated by consuming the body of the god. For all his use of Christian language, Sherrard is offering an understanding of Christianity that is in many respects scarcely orthodox, which sees it more as an esoteric cult than as the culturally inclusive faith of East or West.

That esotericism is apparent when he says that 'certain reservations' must be made about the public doctrine advanced by the Fathers. Not all the doctrine, he claims, was public:

> In keeping with the essentially initiatory and 'closed' character of Christianity, the Christian doctrine, or at least its more important aspects, were reserved for those who were members of the Church – followers, that is, of the Christian Way – and then were only revealed as the aspirants themselves became internally prepared to receive them. In other words, while much of the doctrine is written … other aspects of the doctrine … are the subject of oral, and symbolic, transmission … because in their very nature they cannot be written.[22]

III

This delineation of early Christianity gives Sherrard a position from which to develop his account of the later history of the faith. The decisive moments for him are the conversion of the empire in the fourth century and the break between East and West in the eleventh.

---

22. *Greek East and Latin West*, p. 28.

Sherrard says relatively little in *The Greek East and the Latin West* about the first of these. His focus is on the change from what had been a private, sometimes secret religion of initiates to the established faith of an empire. He points out how ill-fitted Christianity was to take on that role. Unlike Judaism and (later) Islam, it 'possessed no sacred law applicable to every aspect of the social order'.[23] Yet, in the later Western Roman Empire and in Byzantium it had to support a public structure of law such as an empire required. Further, as the normative faith of the whole population, its doctrines had to be presented in a manner accessible to all, and its rituals became public ceremonies. It could no longer be the esoteric cult of a minority: it became an imperial institution, the unique vehicle of salvation holding the keys of the kingdom.

For Sherrard this change was at least deplorable and at worst a betrayal. A religion of inner transformation became a religion of laws and definitions. It fell, he argues, into the hands of rationalists, even if the rationalists were theologians and prelates. However much they formally acknowledged mystery, the norms for the creeds were now reason and conceptual definition. The shift in the Western mind that had begun with Aristotle now enclosed Christianity itself.

It is here that Sherrard finds the roots of the other great crisis in Christian history, the 'schism' of 1054 between East and West. He begins, though, by calling the word 'schism' into question: there can, he claims, be no schism in the Church. For him the Church is a community gathered round the mystery of the Eucharist, and each community is fully the Church because it renews that mystery in its eucharistic life. Only if the Church is conceived of as a corporate institution, a structurally-defined entity in which local churches are 'Church' only to the extent that they belong to that institution, can there be schism.

---

23. *Greek East and Latin West*, p. 46.

With the establishment of Christianity as the imperial religion such an institution was created, based upon hierarchical authority and with the papacy at the apex;[24] and it is within such a Church that Sherrard sees the division as having taken place. He notes the argument that the causes of division were political and cultural, but only to reject it: something more basic was at issue, and that was the understanding of the being of God. Nor could the problem be left to the theology of the cloisters; the Church, as the point of access to salvation was compelled to state its position clearly and publicly in the creeds. Out of that came the *filioque* question. Gradually, from the sixth century, the Latin Church began to add 'and the Son' (*filioque*).

Sherrard's instinct is against such formal declarations; the truth of 'gnosis' infinitely exceeds any verbal definition. But he accepts verbal formulations as pointers, as indicators as to where the truth may be found. To that extent he accepts the eleventh-century arguments. But he remains suspicious of the view that such matters can be resolved by philosophical means, by assimilating them to the domain of rationality; and around the *filioque* he sees the mistaken application of rationalist philosophy to an area in which it did not belong. Seeking as it did to refute heresies that were themselves often rationalisations,

> the Church sought to defend the faith with the definitions of the Councils. But in marking the distinction of its doctrine from the rationalizations by which it felt the faith was threatened, the Church was forced, in order that the distinction should be apparent, to define its dogma in the same kind of language as that in which the heresies

---

24. Sherrard explores the role of the papacy in his *Church, Papacy, and Schism* (London: SPCK, 1978; reprinted Limni, Evia, Greece: Denise Harvey (Publisher), 1996, 2009 and 2024).

themselves were framed; it was forced, that is, to use the language of philosophy.[25]

The doctrines of the Church had now to meet the standards of philosophical argument, of clarity and non-contradiction. But Sherrard is clear that statements of Christian belief are of their nature 'contradictory and paradoxical from the logical point of view, for the simple reason that the Truth is, from the logical point of view, contradictory and paradoxical'.[26]

As well as accepting the test of rationality, there was a narrowing of focus: theology, particularly in the West, 'tended to restrict itself more and more to precisely those existential, Creator-creature relationships' with which the Councils of the fourth and fifth centuries had been concerned. It was of first importance for a Church that presided over the eternal destiny of the people to be clear about how the humanity stood in relation to its creator. But the frame of the debate was too narrow, and the result was a dualism:

> What this meant in effect was, first, that Christian theologians – and, as we shall see, particularly those of the Latin West – tended to become 'locked' in a Creator-creature, Being-and-becoming, dualism which they were incapable of resolving because they failed to recognize any metaphysical and totally unqualified principle by which these two oppositions are transcended.[27]

In that dualistic opposition of creator and creature, Sherrard suggests, God becomes an agent, a being determined by his relation to creation. Defined as creator, God comes to be identified with that role: God is that which brings about all Being as we know it.

---

25. *Greek East and Latin West*, p. 58.
26. Ibid.
27. *Greek East and Latin West*, p. 60.

Ontologically, the distinction between God and Being begins to close. So conceived, God himself

> will be regarded as determined in a more or less absolute sense by the laws of Being; and hence everything, from the first principle down to the last and most contingent details, will be thought of as likewise determined by these laws, and thus deducible in a logically consistent manner.[28]

In such a view, Being comes to contain God, and God becomes subject to whatever laws the rational exploration of Being may establish.[29]

In resisting the reduction of God to Being, Sherrard is not speaking of the being of God. Being – what 'exists' in the usual sense of the word – is the subject of ontology, the philosophy of 'what there is'. God is not a subject of ontology: in that sense he does not exist. His being is not another being among beings; the being of God stands beyond all beings, all that exists.

But something can be said of it through its action in the world. It was around that 'something can be said' that the arguments of the eleventh century grew. What could be said, it was generally agreed, had to do with the persons of the Trinity, their agency as God in the world; and it was there that the *filioque* question arose. Sherrard begins from a position that is classically Orthodox: God, as encountered by humanity, is always encountered in his persons, in the three persons of the Trinity.[30] The persons are in no sense secondary in

---

28. *Greek East and Latin West*, p. 60–1.
29. Sherrard further explores this tendency to place God within the 'laws' of Being in his discussion of René Guénon in 'The Metaphysics of Logic', chapter 4 of *Christianity: Lineaments of a Sacred Tradition* (1998); especially pp. 84 ff.
30. This point is argued, for example, by John Zizioulas, *Being as Communion: Studies in Personhood and the Church* (Crestwood, NY: St Vladimir's Seminary Press, 1997) and by Vladimir Lossky, *The Mystical Theology of the Eastern Church* (Cambridge: James Clarke, 1957), p. 52.

the human experience of God; and to speak of the 'being' of God as prior to the persons, as Western theologians have tended to do, is to miss the point. Personhood, the community of three, is what God *is*. And the persons are known in their particular activity: in the case of the Father, as the 'causal principle'. The person of the Father (his *hypostasis*) is that which 'begets' the Son and from which the Holy Spirit 'proceeds'. To say that the Holy Spirit 'proceeds from the Father *and the Son*' is to confuse the personhoods of the two: the Father as causal principle, the Son as 'eternal Logos'.

This might still invite the question of what God is in himself; and though Sherrard insists that there is no 'prior' to the persons, he allows that the question can still be asked. It is a question about God's essence. Again, Sherrard takes a classical Orthodox view. He states it as follows:

> The Essence of God is totally undetermined and of an absolute simplicity; It can neither be known, divided or communicated, nor can any quality whatever be attributed to It. Therefore, it cannot be called Being, and still less can it be said that It is the cause or principle of being in others.[31]

These restrictions are, in his view, absolute: God in his essence cannot be called creator because that is a determination of the essence (it makes it 'that which creates'), and his essence, unknowable, cannot be determined. What can be said of God can be said only of the persons of the Trinity in their various activities (source of being, saviour, comforter); never of the essence, even though it is what unites the persons in one God.

This establishes the ground for what happened between Eastern and Western churches in the eleventh century. Sherrard traces contrasting tendencies in the theologies of East and West down to that

---

31. *Greek East and Latin West*, p. 65.

point. The theologians of the East placed primary emphasis on the persons, on their real distinction and their multiple activity; that, not in his essence, was how God could be known and spoken of. But the theologians of the West were suspicious of the idea that God might be understood in his distinctions:

> Faced with the Arianism of the Goths and the polytheism of pagan Gaul [they] found it hard to accept a doctrine which appeared to compromise the idea of the essential Unity of God through such emphasis on His multitudinous powers and on the inexhaustible modes of His existence. … In effect, what Western theologians tended increasingly to stress was the idea of the *Summum Ens*, of the absolute One in whom no distinctions of any kind may be admitted.[32]

The Eastern view allowed space for the 'multitudinous powers' and 'modes', and so for the variety of creation. The Western view emphasised an absolute unity of being from which the diversity of creation could only be seen as a falling away. At the same time the priority given to the 'absolute One' with 'no distinctions' tended to dissolve the persons back into the essence, and it became hard to distinguish them. One consequence was the confusion of person-hoods that is reflected in the *filioque*.

Remote and 'theological' though they might seem, these different ways of conceiving of God had consequences for Western culture. In the sixth chapter of *The Greek East and the Latin West*, 'From Theology to Philosophy in the Latin West', Sherrard explores the effect of the Western conception on the place of God in the Western world. In the Eastern view, though God in his essence was unknowable, it was possible to speak of his activity, because God

---

32. *Greek East and Latin West*, p. 67.

was personhood, and it was as persons that the Trinity acts toward the world. But if, as in the West, God is understood primarily as essence, and if there is an insistence on the 'absolute simplicity' and 'indivisibility' of that essence so that there can be no distinction between God and his activity, then it becomes difficult to understand how God can act towards humanity. Such activity compromises his 'absolute simplicity': there is God, and there is what God does, two things. All activity must either dissolve back into the unknowability of the essence, or float free as activity that has no necessary relation to God:

> If no distinction is recognized in God such as that made by the Fathers between the absolute simplicity and indivisibility of his pre-ontological Essence and the multiplicity and divisibility of His ontological powers and energies, what relationship can there be between God and the world? Or what knowledge can man possess either of God, or himself, or of other created things?[33]

Conceiving God as pure and indivisible essence makes it hard to speak of God, and cuts the world, including humanity, loose from this unknowability. The Eastern argument around the *filioque* was a defence of the real distinction between the persons of the Trinity but also of that between God in his being and his creative energies. It is in the multiplicity of his powers that all the variety of creation comes about, and it is because they are his powers that creation can relate to God. The *filioque* argument may seem abstruse; but for Sherrard the medieval weakening of God's personhood began a process that continued in secularism down to the present. God, in the West, became an abstraction, unrelated to humanity and the world.

---

33. *Greek East and Latin West*, p. 143.

IV

The *filioque* dispute and the schism of 1054 were decisive moments in the history of Christianity. But Sherrard traces the source of this division much further back, to the way the theology of Western Christianity had shaped itself. The grounds of the separation were there in Augustine and behind him, once again, was the figure of Aristotle.

The *filioque* had raised questions about the nature of God; and, for Sherrard, that necessarily involved a question about the human capacity for knowledge. As early as 1951, in speaking of St Symeon, he had begun to use the word 'gnosis' for a mode of knowing what was direct and inclusive. Now he takes a phrase from another of the Greek Fathers, St Maximus the Confessor. For a human being to be united to God, Maximus says, it is necessary to have left 'all ideas, reasonings, and even all knowledge and above reason itself, being entirely under the influence of the intellectual sense and having reached the ignorance which is above all knowledge and (what is the same) above every kind of philosophy.'[34] This 'intellectual sense', Sherrard continues, 'is not ... the consequence of any abstract or theoretical speculation'; it is an entry into what is known. Because this intellect, this 'gnosis', has its origin in God, its seeing is itself a union with God. St Gregory Palamas expressed the same understanding: man 'being himself light sees the light with the light'.[35] In an important passage Sherrard comments:

> In such a union, man does not merely contemplate what is outside and beyond himself; he becomes himself what he contemplates, the uncreated ground of his own proper being in which the whole of himself, body and soul, participates,

---

34. *Greek East and Latin West*, p. 140. St Maximus the Confessor, *Ambigua, Patrologia Graeca* 91, 1340A.
35. The ascription is in *Greek East and Latin West*, p. 141n.2.

... by mingling 'unutterably with the light that is above sense and thought'.[36]

This is the heart of what Sherrard means by 'gnosis': a totality of vision by which the human knows itself completely and in that act of knowing is united with the transcendent reality from which its being derives. Without it, humanity is limited to a knowledge of the sensible world that is itself incomplete, and human beings, as incarnations of the divine, are unable to know themselves. This 'intellect' is the presence of God in the human, by which alone the human sees God; it is the light in which the light can be seen. Above Sherrard's grave at Katounia and honouring the light of his intellect, Denise Sherrard inscribed in stone words in Greek from the Psalms: 'in thy light we shall see light'.[37]

It was the loss of any affirmation of this 'intellect' that Sherrard saw as the root of the problems of Western theology. He traces the loss back to the fifth century. Augustine, speaking of what connects the human with God, posited 'the idea of a soul which, in relation to the body, is not only superior to it, but also entirely independent of it'.[38] Only thus could humanity be released from its imprisonment in the material world, and only as soul could human beings inherit eternal life. Sherrard has two difficulties with this. First, it makes the physical aspect of the human subordinate and essentially disposable, not to say evil. Second, he takes issue with Augustine's definition of what it is to be human: 'Man is a rational soul using a body.'[39] For Augustine, the soul is characterised by reason; the body is merely an instrument, mortal and earthly. Man's true self is the rational soul.

---

36. *Greek East and Latin West*, p. 141. The last words are those of Gregory Palamas, in K. Sophocles (ed.) *Gregory Palamas, Twenty-Two Homilies* (Athens, 1861), pp. 170–1.
37. Psalm 36, 9.
38. *Greek East and Latin West*, p. 143.
39. Augustine, *De Moribus ecclesiae*, I. 27. 52. 'Homo igitur, ut homini apparet, anima rationalis est mortali atque terreno utens corpore' (*Greek East and Latin West*, p. 143).

Augustine granted this soul, as Sherrard acknowledges, an intelligence that enables it to know the 'immutable truth which is in God'.[40] What he could not admit was any participation of that intelligence in the being of God of the kind that St Maximus described. On the one hand, that being was unknowable; on the other, the rational soul was created, and nothing created could participate in God's uncreated being. Augustine's denial of any such participation marks, for Sherrard, the beginning of the separation of Western humanity from the divine.

For the moment, though, in Sherrard's discussion of the medieval mind, it is reason that is the issue. Because of Augustine's absolute distinction between the created and the uncreated, between sensible experience and the being of God, and because he characterises the soul in terms of rationality, the ground is set for knowledge to be limited to whatever can be derived rationally from the sensible world. Even though Augustine affirms that 'the human mind, in itself and *a priori*, contains the reflected and created copies of those immutable spiritual essences according to which it itself and everything that is are made',[41] nevertheless these copies are created, reflections and copies only; they allow access of knowledge, but there is no participation.

Sherrard moves from Augustine to Aquinas; and although he notes differences between them, he argues that Aquinas furthers the exclusion of any 'gnosis' of spiritual realities. He does so in his assimilation of Aristotle. Aquinas would have found it unacceptable to follow Augustine in speaking of innate and '*a priori*' copies of eternal forms or essences within the human mind. To accept that would have implied the independent existence of those forms, which Aristotle denied. Just as Aristotle recognised the existence of the forms only in their instantiation in particular entities, so

---

40. *Greek East and Latin West*, p. 143.
41. *Greek East and Latin West*, p. 145.

Aquinas perceived the divine causes of things as existing only in particular acts. Of those humanity might have knowledge; but what humanity could not know were the divine causes, what Sherrard continues to call the forms, that lay behind them. For Aquinas, humanity had no faculty to know such things; the faculty that humanity did possess, the reason, could work only with the material of the sensible world:

> The type of knowledge which Aquinas regards as the highest accessible to man is of quite a different order from that of the 'gnosis' of the Christian Fathers. ... Aquinas regards the direct intuition of divine essences as beyond man's reach; the human intellect as it works in this earthly life can know only by turning to the material and the sensible.[42]

From that sensible experience the best that the human mind is capable of is, as Sherrard puts it echoing one of Aquinas's central terms, 'a mere collection of concepts which may be said to have an analogical likeness to the Divine, but nothing more'.[43]

Nevertheless, there was for Aquinas also revelation. Given the limits of human knowledge, the only way by which divine truths could be known was by God's revelation of them. Reason, observing the sensible world, could not say that Christ was divine, or that the Eucharist communicated his true body. For all doctrine, revelation was the only source. Nor, since revelation was truth, could reason intervene to determine it; what was revealed was revealed. There were now two modes of knowing, revelation of eternal truth and reason working from the evidence of the sensible world. Reason could not operate on revelation; but how did revelation stand in relation to reason?

---

42. *Greek East and Latin West*, p. 150.
43. Ibid.

Sherrard sees two important consequences. First, revelation becomes remote, nothing that we as human beings have any part in: 'the things of faith, which must be believed by all, are equally unknown by all.'[44] Second, an absolute division is made in what the human mind can know. Though revelation has primacy and in principle frames the truths of reason, those truths in practice gain autonomy, are justified within their own sphere. Reason now operates according to its own principles. According to Sherrard, Aquinas brought to completion what had been the tendency of the Western mind since Augustine:

> This divorce of revelation and reason, metaphysics and science, implicit in the philosophy of St Augustine and fully recognized in that of the Scholastics, both indicates to what extent the theoretical basis of the Christian realization was weakened in the West by the nature of much Western medieval theology itself, and also prepared the ground consequently for the whole revolution of thought which was so to modify Western society and culture.[45]

This change has its effect on the kind of questions that human beings ask. 'The metaphysical question, about why things happen, gradually gave place to the "physical" question, about how things happen';[46] and that question came to be answered, more and more, in the scientific terms of causation and mathematics.

The dominance of mathematics as the norm of human knowledge is something that Sherrard will question more than thirty years later in *Human Image: World Image*.[47] Here in *The Greek East and the*

---

44. *Greek East and Latin West*, p. 154.
45. *Greek East and Latin West*, p. 155.
46. *Greek East and Latin West*, p. 156.
47. 'The Fetish of Mathematics and the Iconoclasm of Modern Science', chapter three in Philip Sherrard, *Human Image: World Image* (Ipswich: Golgonooza Press, 1992), pp. 33–55.

Latin West he identifies Descartes as the culmination of the narrowing of the knowable, through his distinction between the world of material entities (*res extensa*) and the world of the mind (*res cogitans*), and in his separation of both from any dependence on God. 'Gnosis' was finally nullified; the grounding for the modern world was in place.

In this discussion of the shaping of the Western mind, Sherrard finds himself describing the loss of any capacity for that total vision that is the culminating possibility of the human. That vision includes the human itself, body as well as spirit; but it also includes all material being in relation to its divine origin. With that capacity gone, human beings are left to inhabit a fragmented world of empirically identified objects; a world in which their own existence as persons and subjects is increasingly under threat.

3

Tradition and Myth

Between the publication of *The Greek East and the Latin West* in 1959 and the mid-1970s Philip Sherrard wrote very little prose of a directly philosophical or theological kind. The argumentative analysis that began in his essays of the late 1940s largely ceases. Not until the publication of *Christianity and Eros* in 1976 and *Church, Papacy, and Schism* in 1978 does that current of his work resume. As is clear from his correspondence with George Seferis, Sherrard was intensely engaged during this decade with translation and publication. The fruits of that effort were the full English versions of Seferis and Cavafy in 1967 and 1972.

Yet, central though that work was, there were other things going on. At the beginning of the decade, in 1960, he published *Athos: The Mountain of Silence*,[1] and that was followed, in 1965, by *Constantinople: Iconography of a Sacred City*.[2] Then, in 1966, there was *Byzantium*,[3] and in 1968 a joint work with John Campbell, *Modern*

---

1. Philip Sherrard, *Athos: The Mountain of Silence* (London: Oxford University Press, 1960). Originally published in German translation by Urs Graf-Verlag Olten, Lausanne and Freiburg, 1959. Referred to subsequently as *Athos*.
2. Philip Sherrard, *Constantinople: Iconography of a Sacred City* (London: Oxford University Press, 1965). Originally published in German translation by Urs Graf-Verlag Olten, Lausanne and Freiburg, 1963. Referred to subsequently as *Constantinople*.
3. Philip Sherrard, *Byzantium* (Netherlands: Time Inc., 1966). Referred to subsequently as *Byzantium*.

Greece.[4] These volumes involved extensive scholarly reading. Alongside his translation work, Sherrard was making his fullest engagement with the Greek inheritance that passed, crucially for him, through the Byzantine years. At the core of his interest is tradition. He had spoken in his 1948 essay of Seferis's power to enter 'the abyss of history';[5] in these writings of the 1960s Sherrard makes his own descent, drawing from it, as Seferis had, an ever fuller image of what it is to be human. Though in speaking of Athos and Constantinople he may appear simply to be describing or narrating, his detailed delineation of their life is an entry into the totality of those worlds, a weighing of their ability to contain a full vision of the human.

As a point of entry Sherrard often uses contemporary voices. He supports his own accounts with extensive quotations from writers of the time, and tradition is made to speak. This has the effect of bringing the past directly before the reader and of rooting Sherrard's commentary in the tradition he is describing. Part of that tradition, and a central dynamic in the worlds of Athos and Byzantium, is myth.

I

In December 1952 Sherrard delivered the Koraes Lecture at King's College, London. His subject was General Makriyannis, the independence fighter and chronicler of the Greek War of Independence. In his lecture Sherrard said: 'The original expression of the psychological background of a people, of their feeling for life, is myth. Myth is, as it were, the projection of the subconscious aspirations of a people, the way through which a people becomes conscious of its historical destiny, of its own latent powers.'[6] Much of Sherrard's

---

4. John Campbell and Philip Sherrard, *Modern Greece* (New York: Frederick Praeger: Ernest Benn, 1968).
5. *Blood and Light* 63.
6. 'General Makriyannis: The Portrait of a Greek', reprinted in Philip Sherrard, *The Wound of Greece* (New York: St Martin's Press, 1979), pp. 54–5.

understanding of myth is there in this passage. As a narrative form, it is a way of knowing and expressing identity and meaning; for some kinds of meaning, those that reach furthest into human identity, the only way of knowing and expressing. Sherrard does not limit 'myth' to collections of ancient tales, and to identify a narrative or cultural practice as myth is not to depreciate it. It is rather to say that myth, speaking as it does from the 'abyss of history', may communicate a deep human truth.

For Sherrard, the worlds of Athos and Byzantium are worlds grounded in myth. Athos lives from the Christian myth, the Narrative of revelation and salvation. Constantinople is a *civitas*, an organic urban reality, that seeks to realise a myth, that of union between the secular Empire and the heavenly New Jerusalem. Those who live in those worlds live through those myths; myths live through participation. When that participation ceases, myths die.

Sherrard's account of Athos (which he visited for the first time in April 1951) explores such dimensions of myth and participation. There is the monastic life itself, the life of withdrawal and transformation, its meaning dependent on the Christian myth, on the possibility of moving to transcendence through discipline and contemplation. In that sense the whole monastic project is deeply mythical. Sherrard's readiness to enter the constitutive myth is apparent in his dealing with the founding narratives of Athos. He quotes extensively from the life of Peter the Athonite, by tradition the first hermit to settle on Athos in the ninth century. The place is chosen for him by the Mother of God. Having escaped from Arab capture in Syria, and sailing, as he planned, for Palestine, he is miraculously delayed close to Mount Athos:

A light sleep came upon the God-bearing Peter. And he saw the most pure Mother of God appearing in exceeding glory and the great Nicholas with veneration, fear and modesty approaching her, and saying to her in supplication: 'Mistress and Lady of all, since it was your will to free this your servant from that wretched captivity mercifully show him also a place in which to spend the rest of his life, practising what is lovable to God.' And, turning, the Mother of God said to him: 'His rest shall be on the Mountain of Athos.'[7]

Sherrard presents this and similar stories without comment. In part, he is simply recording what Athos is, what has traditionally been said of it. But there is also a delicacy toward myth itself. To speak of the Virgin giving directions, or of icons that floated across the waves, is to enter a realm of meaning beyond the normal constraints. For Sherrard, the necessary recognition is that the truth of myth is revealed only through participation. The monks of Athos know the truth of the Christian myth by living within it. To make myth an object of rational knowledge – did it happen or not? – is at once to drain it of its meaning. Myth can be understood only if there is an initial concession on the part of the hearer, a lowering of defences, an openness to other modes of truth.

Sherrard makes a parallel point about the liturgical life of the monasteries. Grounded in contemplation, repetitive, almost mechanical as they are, the daily rituals create a deep participation, transform the relationship between knower and known. Through habitual discipline and 'recollectedness', the monk 'is brought into the right frame of mind for the next stage, that in which object and subject, the formal act and the spiritual content, begin to flow together without break'.[8] There is an approach to a unified vision.

It is withdrawal from participation, both as a way of living and knowing, that makes Sherrard suspicious of the increasingly

---

7. Sherrard (*Athos*, p. 6) is quoting from the 'Life of Peter the Athonite', in Kirsopp Lake, *The Early Days of Monasticism on Mount Athos* (Oxford: The Clarendon Press, 1909).

8. *Athos*, p. 81.

idiorhythmic mode of Athonite life. Instead of living as hermits or in monastic communities, he saw monks living essentially private lives, in their own quarters and with their own possessions. For Sherrard, that was a resurgence of individualism, a withdrawal from the participation that was the essence of monasticism. Its effect was to reduce the monasteries to cultural curiosities, to exotic destinations for the inquisitive tourist.

Yet, he believes that, even in the 1960s, the goal of this life has not wholly been lost. The monk's end is deification: to be united with God just as God is united with humanity in the Incarnation. This objective, 'to become God', strange and even blasphemous in the ears of Western Christianity, is the final participation, that mutuality with the divine towards which the whole course of monastic life is directed. Sherrard traces it through the stages of repentance and purification, of silence, sobriety and prayer, to the ultimate union:

> Sobriety and prayer lead ... not only to the perception and enjoyment of divine realities, but to union with the Divine itself. And in this union ... man is resurrected to, or renewed in, that state for which he was created 'in the beginning'. He achieves his 'deification' and becomes himself God-like.[9]

This was not an abstract spiritualisation, a sterile denaturing of the human but its rich fulfilment. Sherrard demonstrates that in a quotation from St Symeon the New Theologian. He responds particularly to the physicality of Symeon's language, to its personal directness:

> If you wish you will become [Christ's] limb,
> and thus the limbs of every one of us

---

9. *Athos*, p. 102.

become the limbs of Christ and Christ our very limbs;
and all the ugly, graceful will become,
clothed with heavenly loveliness and splendour,
and we become as Gods with God united.[10]

II

These themes, of myth and participation, continue in Sherrard's *Constantinople* of 1965. To them is added the theme of the icon, both as sacred image and as a way of understanding Byzantine civilisation as a whole.

Sherrard's depth of acquaintance with the Byzantine world, already apparent in *Athos*, is even clearer in *Constantinople*. He was confident of his expertise in that area. Later, in 1967, he applied (unsuccessfully) for the chair of Byzantine and Modern Greek literature at Oxford; and, asking Seferis in a letter for his support, said that it was 'a subject that I do know something about (at least, I don't know of any English person who knows more about it'.[11] Primary Byzantine sources, travellers' records and modern scholarship are all extensively used; and, as in *Athos*, Sherrard includes contemporary voices speaking from within the tradition.

If Athonite monasticism aimed at an individual goal, the unification of the soul with God, in *Constantinople* Sherrard presents a communal goal, the transformation of the human *civitas* into the Kingdom. He sets out the two mythic structures that governed the life of the Byzantine Empire. The first, asserted in Constantine's insistence on continuity with Rome, was the myth of rational public order that had governed Old Rome; this is what Sherrard had described in *The Greek East and the Latin West* as Ciceronian humanism,

---

10. Sherrard's translation in *Athos*, p. 104. No direct reference is given.
11. *Blood and Light*, p. 320. Though he failed to secure the Oxford chair, Sherrard was successful two years later when he was appointed lecturer in the History of the Orthodox Church at King's College, London, a post he held until 1977.

a civic faith in the discourse of education and reason. It was the task of the emperor to sustain rational order through his power and the institutions of the state. Sherrard shows how orderly Constantinople was in that respect. There were the elaborate ceremonies that ritualised all imperial activity, and there was the structuring of economic life through a system of craft guilds and state procurement. Despite its frequent violence and cruelty, the Byzantine state never quite lost the belief that it was the model of all earthly governance, the destined order for humanity.

But the mythic ambition reached higher. Besides the myth of New Rome there was the myth of New Jerusalem, of a divine order reflected if not consummated in the state. 'The Empire was to be a worldly instrument in the hand of God for the realization of his purpose.'[12] Within that narrative the Emperor, the *basileus*, was more than the custodian of the *civitas*: he was the point of intersection of the earthly and the heavenly. Though not a priest nor supreme in the religious hierarchy (that place belonged to the Patriarch) he was nevertheless pivotal in the relation of earth to heaven. Sherrard expresses that in his own terms. 'The *basileus* himself is regarded as providing a link, a bridge between [earth and heaven]. The *basileus* is a symbol of the cosmic king, the hieratic figure in whom is embodied a mythical or mystic sense of the incorporation of a ray of the divine Logos, Heaven's King.'[13] If not a priest then certainly hieratic, priestly; his were the hands that God had entrusted with his world.

None of that would have been conceivable had there not been a confidence that the material and temporal world, the world of power and the market, could participate in the life of a transcendent order. Just as the discipline and ritual of Athos made possible participation in the divine being, so the life of the city, worldly as well

---

12. *Constantinople*, p. 44.
13. *Constantinople*, p. 44.

as hieratically, was a participation in that which transcended it. In that life everything could be gathered:

> Arabian acrobats dance on a rope, Indians parade an elephant. A court dignitary, in costume of brocaded silk, passes on horseback, a long cortège behind him. A procession files past. ... Students from the Imperial University turned over books in the book-vendors' stalls set up in front of the Basilica. ... A carriage drawn by four white horses, their harness encrusted with gold and silver ... passes a lumbering Scythian coach, its passengers clothed in skins.[14]

Everything human, for virtue or for vice, was there; Constantinople was a real city. But there was something else:

> Everywhere within this intense and continuous movement were pools of quiet, centres of withdrawal within the city's maelstrom, enclosed spaces free from prying eye and extraneous distraction, given over to the practice of prayer and contemplation. ... Here in cloister and walled garden the liberating round of the monastic discipline continued day and night at the very heart of the city, perpetual reminder of the superb vanity of the spectacle which ran its mundane course outside their gates.[15]

Yet, for Sherrard, this contrast is not a contradiction. Both are humanly required; each needs the other as they challenge each other. With an eye to the lack of anything comparable in the modern West, Sherrard insists on the necessity of that challenge. Speaking of the raw humanity of the city, he says:

---

14. *Constantinople*, p. 14.
15. *Constantinople*, p. 14.

It is precisely when it is challenged in this way, at its very heart, that this spectacle, this collective expression of the human ego, achieves, as at Constantinople, the quality of a moving pageant or of a dance renewed continually on the brink of its own denial. Where this ever-present repudiation of its most cherished claims ... is banished from the city, as it is banished from the modern city, then the spectacle of the city's life itself sinks to the ultimate drabness of an army-camp whose pleasure- or profit-bound conscripts gyrate in the vortex of their own soul-destroying fatuity.[16]

Not for the only time, in *Constantinople*, Sherrard's language recalls Yeats: there is gyration, there is a dance, one that unites and vivifies and yet transcends all Yeats's 'mere complexities' of human lives.[17]

The citizens of Constantinople were participants in both realities – the material kingdom and the spiritual kingdom. In the conjunction of the two myths, Byzantium held for Sherrard the promise of a unifying vision. He makes the contrast with the modern city:

We have become so used to looking upon a city merely as a more or less haphazard accumulation of buildings and persons gathered together into one locality in response to economic or social pressures, expressive of no doctrine, ignorant of metaphysics, its inhabitants united by nothing except a common allegiance to their particular self-interests, that the notion that a city may come into being and develop as the organic manifestation of certain coherent and predetermined values is practically inconceivable.[18]

---

16. Ibid.
17. Not surprisingly, the poems that Sherrard echoes in this book are 'Byzantium' and 'Sailing to Byzantium'.
18. *Constantinople*, p. 37.

The modern city is fragmented, a conjunction of accidents without unity. For Sherrard, Constantinople was a city 'in which are concentrated and from which radiate the inner "motive-forces", the dynamic forms, of a particular vision of human life and its destiny'.[19]

Myth and participation in myth: these Sherrard finds in the thousand years of Byzantium, but there is a further dimension. He gives his book the subtitle *Iconography of a Sacred City*. From that the reader might expect a descriptive survey of the city in its characteristic artistic forms, perhaps in the manner of Ruskin's *The Stones of Venice*.[20] And there is, of course, something of that; no account of a city as visual as Constantinople could ignore what would have met the eye.

But Sherrard has a deeper point. The iconography is of the city itself: the city itself is an icon. In its fusion of the two myths of empire and kingdom, the city does what icons do – embody transcendence in materiality. Icons are the material actualisation of participation, of the earthly in the heavenly and the heavenly in the earthly, with no separation. The icon is one; not a reference to another reality but that reality present in the material object.

Sherrard says little directly about icons in either *Athos* or *Constantinople*. His fullest discussion comes almost thirty years later, in chapter six, 'The Art of the Icon', of *The Sacred in Life and Art*.[21] Even there he offers nothing in the way of definition; his emphasis is on context, on the liturgical life within which the icon finds its place. He is hostile to the idea of the icon as a work of art, detachable from its intended setting. In essence, his approach in 1965 is the same; what makes Constantinople an icon is the totality of its life,

---

19 Ibid.

20. Sherrard covers much of that in *Byzantium*, a book directed more to the general reader, particularly the sections on the typical arrangement of images in a church (*Byzantium*, 101–11) and on the visual arts (*Byzantium*, 145–59).

21. Philip Sherrard, *The Sacred in Life and Art* (Ipswich: Golgonooza Press, 1990), pp. 68–84.

the context of living where all its art is held. Insofar as he speaks of individual artefacts he prefers the language of symbol, but the point is the same – the simultaneity of materiality and transcendence. His most striking example is architectural. He asks what image would most immediately have engaged the visitor to the city, and his answer is the dome of St Sophia. That enormous dome was, in constructional terms, the solution to a physical problem, how to enclose and unify a large space. But it went beyond that:

> It was a desire to make visible a certain complex of ideas, to express in such intelligible symbolism a certain vision of reality, and not any structural and utilitarian interest in a means of covering space that impelled Justinian ... to give such prominence and importance to the dome. ... It was, in terms we have already used, the animated house of the Divinity, the living temple of the Logos, replica of heaven upon earth.[22]

The dome with its mosaic of the Pantocrator makes physical Christ's relation to the world: 'it was his divine presence that animated the space of the dome, so that in this way it became the seat of his celestial authority and compassion, image of the radiant heavens to which man aspired from the darkness in which he lived on earth below.'[23] The material shares in the transcendent, and those who see it are not simply onlookers: they participate in what they see.

III

That participation is Sherrard's model for all art. In the mid-1960s, following the publication of *Athos* and *Constantinople*, he was

----

22. *Constantinople*, pp. 38–9.
23. *Constantinople*, p. 39.

primarily engaged with translation of the poetry of Seferis and Cavafy, work carried out in collaboration with the American scholar Edmund Keeley. They had already published an anthology of modern Greek poetry in translation; now they undertook the heavier task of preparing English-language collections of these poets' works.[24] Both names were known in the English-speaking world; both had already been translated, not least by Sherrard himself. There was an audience, but there was also a personal involvement, an engagement with this poetry.

As far as Seferis is concerned, Sherrard's essay of 1948, with its high estimation of Seferis compared with the English-language poetry of the time, helps to explain the personal importance.[25] Material from the 1960s adds little to that. Part of the problem is the absence of critical material in the volumes of translation. There is a brief 'Foreword', written in 1966 and repeated in the later editions of Seferis's *Collected Poems*; they are brief because Seferis himself insisted that there should be no extended critical introduction. In a letter to Edmund Keeley, he had objected to a draft of a fuller critical introduction, saying 'I believe that appreciations of the poet in this book are redundant. There you must limit yourself to your role of translators'.[26] Sherrard seems to have taken that to heart; apart from the briefest of contexts, there are no critical introductions to his translations.

However, on 21 September 1971 Seferis died; and the following year Sherrard wrote a full appraisal for *The London Magazine*.[27] This

24. Keeley and Sherrard's anthology, *Six Poets of Modern Greece*, appeared in 1960; their first edition of *George Seferis: Collected Poems, 1924–1955* in 1967; their *C. P. Cavafy: Selected Poems* in 1972, and their *Collected Poems* in 1975.
25. *Blood and Light* 56–74.
26. Letter to Edmund Keeley of 18 September 1966. Quoted *Blood and Light*, footnote to page 313.
27. 'George Seferis 1900–1971: The Man and his Poetry', *The London Magazine*, October/November 1972. Reprinted in Philip Sherrard, *The*

article, in large part a retrospective of a friendship that had started with Sherrard's first letter of February 1947, gives a direct sense of Seferis's personal importance to him, not least through his choice of the poems he discusses.

Almost half the material Sherrard quotes is from Seferis's early poem of 1933–4, 'Mythistorema'. The title is a coinage; in it myth and history are fused together. There is history, including Seferis's memory of his own exile, of his family's expulsion from Smyrna in 1922; but there is also Orestes wandering in banishment and the Argonauts struggling with the waves. Seferis, like Sherrard, saw myth as a central mode of human understanding and, again like Sherrard, he resisted the rationalist impulse to separate myth and history. For both, myth and history are knowledge, part of that common awareness on which humanity is based. After Sherrard's exploration of the workings of myth within Byzantine civilisation, that was a profound connection.

But there was more. At the outset of the 1971 *London Magazine* article Sherrard set out a test, one that he applies implicitly to all art: it should be 'one further testimony to man's great struggle to prevent human life and civilization itself from sinking into turpitude, inertia and spiritual death'.[28] For Sherrard, that was Seferis's achievement; and to that he brought extraordinary resources.

There was, first and most immediately, the physicality of the poetry, the materiality of its engagement with the world. 'It is full of the smell of tar and the taste of brine and salt, of old ports, of old ships … it is full of the sea and the people of the sea.'[29] This 'vivid sense of the physical world' is, for Sherrard, more than colour, more than sensory enrichment. In it he sees a mind that has escaped the Aristotelian divorce 'between man's soul and his natural environ-

---

Wound of Greece: Studies in Neo-Hellenism (London: Collings, 1978), pp. 94–117. Referred to subsequently as *Wound of Greece*.
28. *Wound of Greece*, p. 94.
29. *Wound of Greece*, p. 95.

ment', the separation that he had traced in *The Greek East and the Latin West*. There is in Seferis

> a sense that nature – the created world, including man's own physical existence – is rooted in the metaphysical world. ...
> It is a sense that man should harmonize himself with the natural world and respect it, rather than set himself apart from it or rather than subject the natural world to some discipline, scientific or economic.[30]

This metaphysical rooting emerges from the physicality, from the material immediacy. In one of his rare Buddhist references, Sherrard quotes the Japanese poet Mstsuo Bashō: 'Go to the pine if you want to learn about the pine, or to the bamboo if you want to learn about the bamboo ... you must leave your subjective preoccupation with yourself. Otherwise you impose yourself on the object and do not learn'.[31]

Seferis can stand before the objects of the world and let them speak. But he also intuits a further reality: there is the knowing that precedes conceptualisation. That, for Sherrard, is the source of Seferis's sensitivity to what hovers at the limit of vision, 'those inner sources of vitality – sources which everyday preoccupations so easily obscure and overlay'. There is also in Seferis 'a sense of some deep loss, as if man's life had been torn with violence from its natural setting.'[32] Both infuse the texture of the verse and give it a metaphysical depth. That loss, which Seferis knew most vividly in 1922, finds its fullest expression in the late poem 'The King of Asine', in its reaching out for an unreachable that is also the most necessary:

---

30. *Wound of Greece*, p. 110.
31. (*Wound of Greece*, p. 110). This saying is frequently repeated in most accounts of Bashō, but Sherrard's source is unclear.
32. *Wound of Greece*, pp. 110–11.

And the poet lingers, looking at the stones, and asks himself
  does there really exist.

among these ruined lines, edges, points, hollows and curves
  does there really exist.

here where one meets the path of rain, wind and ruin.

does there exist the movement of the face, shape of the
  tenderness

of those who have shrunk so strangely in our lives.[33]

Seferis is reaching for the reality behind a name that is all that is left in Homer's record; behind the name there is more, the indefinable, that meets the need for love.

This need is most nearly satisfied in Seferis's images of return. At the end of this essay, Sherrard turns again to myth and imagines, 'the metaphysical experience of an Oedipus who, after much suffering, after many blind journeys, descends at last living into the earth that "receives him mercifully" and returns him to the Great Mother of Rebirth'.[34] He finds return and perhaps rebirth in another of Seferis's later poems, 'Memory II':

So I continued along the dark path
And turned into my garden and dug and buried the reed
And again I whispered: some morning the resurrection will
  come,
Dawn's light will blossom red as trees glow in spring,
The sea will be born again, and the wave will again fling-forth
  Aphrodite.
We are the seed that dies. And I entered my empty house.

---

33. *Wound of Greece*, p. 113.
34. *Wound of Greece*, p. 114.

Sherrard's attachment to Seferis derives from a common investment in tradition and myth, from a shared openness to the metaphysical. The roots of his engagement with Cavafy are more difficult
to trace. After the discussion in chapter three of *The Marble Threshing
Floor* in 1959, there is little further commentary. There he values
Cavafy's honesty, his recognition of the futility of a life lived solely
on the level of the aesthetic. Cavafy demonstrates how 'the aesthetic
world, being divorced from any principle, is a world of disorder,
uncertainty, and despair. It is a doomed world. It is subject to
attacks, against which it is powerless, both from without and
within.'[35] But, for Sherrard, this demonstration is also a limitation.
The 'principle' that is lacking is any secure metaphysical base.
Without that, all that is left is disorder and futility. The mood and
tone of Cavafy's poetry brilliantly display that, and they win
Sherrard's admiration. But Cavafy has no weapon against his
despair. All he can do is explore the pathos of a condition infected
by 'the terrible transience of all to which its affections are attached'.[36]
Unlike Seferis, Cavafy lacks the intuition of any secure ground.

Those comments are from the 1950s, from Sherrard's PhD years.
From the years of translation there is no critical commentary. It is
probably fair to say that, for all Sherrard's respect as a translator,
Cavafy meant rather less to him than Seferis. In some respects that
might be hard to explain. Cavafy was, after all, deeply conscious of
tradition, of 'the abyss of history', and of how myth can permeate
lives. Compared with Seferis, however, tradition and myth play a
very different role in his poetry. For Cavafy, they are an area in which
a particular sensibility can exercise itself, a sensibility that Sherrard
had described as one of aesthetic irony. The inheritance of myth and
tradition makes the present ironic, suffuses it with loss and nos-
talgia; instead of feeding the present, myth and tradition stand at a

---

35. *Marble Threshing*, p. 101.
36. *Marble Threshing*, p. 117.

distance as the reference points for the irony. In a paradoxical way, Cavafy's poetry, nostalgic and myth-filled as it is, is a poetry of the present, of the moment of its own realisation. It is less truly invested in its past than the poetry of Seferis. And if Seferis's use of myth sometimes points to liberation, Cavafy's carries with it closure and confinement, in a world where myth is part of the furniture of regret.

IV

At the end of the previous decade, in 1959, Sherrard had published his long critique of the working of reason in the Western mind. Largely negative in tone, it hardly suggested where remedies might lie to the West's alienation, to the confinement of knowledge within the bounds of rationalism. His pessimism is well expressed in the 'Epilogue' to *The Greek East and the Latin West*, where he questions whether things may have come full circle, whether the contemporary West might be in the same state as the Roman world at the time of Cicero, when reason was seen as the only bulwark against chaos. Perhaps, he felt, things might be even worse now: 'the 'paganism' of the modern West would seem to be of a lower order than that of the Hellenistic and Roman world: it is both more general, and more exclusively materialist.'[37] Against that, in 1959, he had set tradition, and Christianity as '*the* spiritual tradition of the West', the only surviving resource for a different image of the human.

Sherrard's work in the 1960s, both his cultural studies and his translation, looks towards the recovery of tradition. There was the myth-centred life of Byzantium. There was Seferis's power to make myth a feeder for the present.

But neither tradition nor myth can be known without participation. Without it tradition becomes little more than a tourist display; and myth without participation becomes failed explanation,

---

37. *Greek East and Latin West*, p. 196.

relegated to the data of anthropology. As Sherrard moves into the 1970s, participation and mutuality become ever more vital, of body with spirit in *Christianity and Eros* and of Church with world in *Church, Papacy, and Schism.*

4

Against Dualism

Sherrard published two books in the 1970s – *Christianity and Eros* in 1976[1] and *Church, Papacy, and Schism* in 1978.[2] Both are short studies, the first of the Christian attitude to sexuality, and the second of ecclesiology, of the Roman Church as it formed itself around the papacy. Both grew out of Sherrard's dissatisfaction with Western Christianity, already evidenced in his essays of the 1950s and in *The Greek East and the Latin West*. *Church, Papacy, and Schism* might even be seen as an extended footnote to his analysis of the Constantinian Church and its medieval development, already outlined in *The Greek East and the Latin West*.

In both books the value of participation holds centre stage. In his studies of Athos and Byzantium participation had a social aspect: the monk shared in the life of the monastery, the citizens of the empire shared in the life of the sacred *civitas*. Now his concern is more individual: with sexuality as the primary human participation, biological but also spiritual, and with the degree to

---

1. Philip Sherrard, *Christianity and Eros: Essays on the Theme of Sexual Love* (London: SPCK, 1976; reprinted Limni, Evia, Greece: Denise Harvey (Publisher), 1995, 2002 and 2022). Referred to subsequently as *Christianity and Eros*.
2. Philip Sherrard, *Church, Papacy, and Schism: A Theological Enquiry* (London: SPCK, 1978; reprinted Limni, Evia, Greece: Denise Harvey (Publisher), 1996 and 2009). Referred subsequently as *Church, Papacy, Schism*.

85

which the Church makes real a participation of the spirit. In both he sees failure: spirituality denies sexuality, and the Church offers moral principles governing a grudgingly acknowledged carnal necessity.

But the enemy of participation is dualism, and that is Sherrard's target in these books. In *Christianity and Eros* it is the endemic dualism of spirit and body in the Christian tradition. In *Church, Papacy, and Schism* it is the dualism of Church and world. Both work against any unity of vision. The first creates a doubleness in human self-understanding; the second casts the believer into a conflict of unreconciled realities, of the material world of science and an 'other world' that increasingly floats free into abstraction.

Besides these two books there is a shorter text from the 1970s that explores dualism in a different context. In 1975 Sherrard published an essay, *W. B. Yeats and the Search for Tradition*.[3] This, an extended discussion of an English-language poet, is a rarity in Sherrard's writing, but the reason for his valuing Yeats is clear. Yeats, like Sherrard, was a searcher for a unifying vision. Like Sherrard, he saw tradition and myth as vital resources in that effort. But he too was threatened by dualisms: of the real and the imagined, of past and present. Sherrard's discussion dissects those pressures and makes an assessment of how far Yeats reached his vision of unity.

Dualism, duality, unity: these words have a complicated relationship in Sherrard's writing. It is clear that dualism is the enemy and that the goal is unity, a unifying vision. But he is not aiming at some homogeneity of being, at a monistic state in which all that exists is essentially one. His rejection of that is clear from his treatment of the Vedanta in chapter three of *Human Image: World Image*. There is real differentiation in being, and differentia-tion – the reality of different existents – is what makes the

---

3. Philip Sherrard, *W. B. Yeats and the Search for Tradition* (Ipswich: Golgonooza Press, 1975). Referred to subsequently as *Yeats*.

magnificence of the world. Duality understands that there is this and there is that. How important this was for Sherrard is clear from some words that he wrote to George Katsimbalis in an early letter of 7 August 1950:

> If 'the Greek Soul' is anything it is something of great diversity, not an identity. It is feminine as well as masculine, apophatic as well as cataphatic. It is the tension between these contradictions which give Greek poetry much of its pathos. If, in the name of orthodoxy, you try to banish or suppress one of these poles you will only in the end castrate your creative life. The creative life depends upon the interplay of these opposites and contradictions: it depends upon keeping them active, and letting them germinate their own rhythms.[4]

I

Christianity and Eros begins with an image of the perfection of sexual love. For Sherrard, it is a love that includes and transcends what he calls its 'carnal (or genital) expression' by being 'a mutual awareness and recognition which is a total act of the soul'; it is a love in which the distinction between *agape* and *eros* is transcended, in which 'the fully differentiated beings of man and woman' merge without ever being lost. He admits that such fullness of sexual love is very rare; he illustrates it from literary examples, Tristan and Iseult, Dante and Beatrice, Zhivago and Lara in *Doctor Zhivago.*[5]

In what is often an angry book; Sherrard argues that Christianity as a whole and Western Christianity in particular have constantly forced dualisms upon this most participatory of human experiences. Although churches East and West have formally acknowledged

---

4. Initially published in Avi Sharon (ed.) 'The Light and the Blood', *Arion*, (Boston) 7 (1) 1999, p. 67. Reprinted in *Blood and Light*, p. 360.
5. *Christianity and Eros*, pp. 1–3.

marriage as a sacrament (calling in evidence Christ's miracle at Cana), they have also been deeply uncomfortable with sexuality: 'the attitude of Christian thought towards the sexual relationship and its spiritualizing potentialities has been in practice singularly limited and negative.'[6] Celibacy, following St Paul, has been seen as a 'higher' state than marriage; and, although marriage is acknowledged as having biblical validation, there has been a darker judgement beneath the surface. It is there in early Christian theologians, even in those whom Sherrard normally admires, such as St Gregory of Nyssa and St Maximus the Confessor:

> Although precluded by their basic doctrine from subscribing to an out-and-out dualism in this matter, and so from attributing the origin of sexuality directly to an evil power, their practical attitude differs little from dualists of a Manichaean type. Sexuality is tainted. It is impure. … If not actually evil in itself, its use stirs up the passions and so leads directly to sin. It is the springhead through which the tribes of evil pour into human nature.[7]

In practice, the Eastern and Western versions of Christianity reach much the same negative conclusion as far as sexuality is concerned. The anthropology of the Eastern Church understands man as created 'in the image' of God, and hence in essence as pure spirit (*pneuma*) and intellect (*nous*). Man's 'animal' nature, including sexuality, is the consequence of the Fall. In the West the 'animal' nature is primary; it is that which is to be overcome through salvation in Christ. Whether primary or secondary, pre- or post-lapsarian, in neither case is sexuality part of the perfect humanity that God intended.[8]

---

6. *Christianity and Eros*, p. 4.
7. *Christianity and Eros*, p. 5.
8. *Christianity and Eros*, pp. 5–9.

Consequently, Christianity is inclined to see sexuality as a concession to human imperfection, even to the inevitability of sin. At its most extreme this thinking has been applied to the very existence of two sexes:

> Even the distinction between man and woman only exists or is only established because God foresees that man is going to sin and so to fall and therefore will be in need of a mode of propagation which will make it possible for him to continue the human race under new conditions.[9]

God bends towards human weakness, but there is a price to be paid: sexual love is 'at the expense of the spiritual life'. Out of this negativity there arises a pervasive confusion about the place of sexuality in human experience, a confusion still detectable in the later twentieth century in the encyclical letter *Humanae Vitae*.[10] On the one hand marriage is to be esteemed and given the status of a sacrament, and yet its basis, the sexual act, is granted only conditional approval. Since the end of marriage is, in this view, procreation, and since sexuality is required for procreation, sexuality is justified to the extent that procreation is its aim. However, sexuality itself remains in question, and marriage is set on a dubious foundation. When procreation is not the end, or is artificially prevented, then sexuality is once more seen as animal imperfection, as the enemy of the spirit. What neither Eastern nor Western Christianity has been able to sustain, Sherrard believes, is a truly sacramental understanding of marriage, in which marriage as a sacrament transforms the being of those who participate in it, spiritually and physically. If the Church offers, as it does, the relationship between Christ and his Church as its image of marriage,

---

9. *Christianity and Eros*, p. 7.
10. Encyclical letter of Pope Paul VI, 1968, *Humanae Vitae*. Available on the Vatican website, https://www.vatican.va

if the symbolism of Christ and the Church applied to marriage is to have a creative or spiritualizing influence on marriage, it must be recognised that the relationship between man and woman is capable of being transformed into an eternal and metaphysical bond. ... The relationship between man and woman must be recognized as possessing *a priori* this metaphysical and sacramental potentiality.[11]

That recognition, Sherrard believes, has always been withheld, often using Jesus's words in support: 'For in the resurrection they neither marry, nor are given in marriage, but are as the angels of God in heaven'.[12]

The consequences of that withholding are, Sherrard believes, visible in the contemporary world. Because the Western Church made procreation defining of marriage, and because sexual intercourse is required for procreation, the act of intercourse itself, of 'consummation', became definitive for marriage. This view

pretends that it is the mere act of coition in itself which ... confirms and consummates the marriage sacrament, irrespective of the degree and quality of the individual participation of the man and woman concerned and of whether in other respects their relationship is one which justifies it in the first place.[13]

This paradoxical emphasis, on a physical act, which is at the same time spiritually suspect, has had an influence in Western culture well beyond the bounds of the Church. The sexual act has been overvalued and, Sherrard suggests, 'hopelessly idealized', removed from its setting in the fullness of a relationship. If sexuality has been

11. *Christianity and Eros*, p. 14.
12. Matthew 22:30.
13. *Christianity and Eros*, p. 29.

debased in the contemporary world, Christianity may have prepared the way for that.

Sherrard's argument is for an integrated, unitary view of human nature, one in which both body and spirit find their place. Once they are set against each other the door is open to the contradictions that permeate Christian thinking and the confusions of the contemporary world. But the roots of the body-spirit dualism lie deeper than the question of sexuality. They originate in an image of the human. Much Christian thinking, Sherrard believes, has been infected by a dualistic anthropology, an alien model that carries traces of Gnosticism and Manichaeism:

> It is quite clear that the notion that man is really a bodiless spirit or soul who has been embodied temporarily as a result of the fall, and even as a punishment for falling, so that salvation consists in freeing the soul from the body and discarnating, is no part of Christian doctrine. ... Man's reality is an embodied reality, and so much is this the case that for him to think or attempt to act as though he possesses a soul apart from a body is to cripple his nature at its roots.[14]

What makes such a dualistic view impossible for Christianity is the Incarnation; this 'discarnating' of humanity's 'embodied reality' is a denial of Christianity's foundational truth.

The great corrective, Sherrard believes, is simply to acknowledge what we are: 'man must start from where he is and with what he is capable of experiencing and grow from that.' There is no point in devising spiritualised anthropologies that ignore our own nature. Where sexuality is denied, the alternative has too often been 'the weary negation of pretending to be bodiless and sexless, and of suppressing desire until it is believed to have been killed off'.

---

14. *Christianity and Eros*, p. 41.

Exiled from the domain of the properly human, '[desire] can only fester and breed ever more deformed creatures after its own distorted image: Caliban begetting Calibans.'[15]

In the later part of *Christianity and Eros* Sherrard explores some semi-mythical accounts of sexuality and its origins: the idea, for example, to be found in some of the Greek Fathers, that the human being was first created in an androgyne, sexless form, and that sexuality was a consequence of the Fall. He considers, too, a group of Russian thinkers who, in the late nineteenth and early twentieth centuries, developed their own accounts: sexuality as the fracturing of an original completeness, as the place where, through ascetic self-denial, egoism can be overcome. The ideas of Soloviev, Merezhkovsky and Berdyaev clearly intrigue him, partly because of their use of what is in effect myth; that appeals to his conviction that myth extends the human capacity for knowledge. But in the end he finds them still infected by the underlying dualisms, one of which is that of male and female, with women given a secondary status.

Christianity and Eros was written at broadly the same time as the essays that Sherrard would publish later in *The Rape of Man and Nature*. Already in his discussion of sexuality it is possible to see a movement to the central concern of his later writing, the realisation of a true image of the human. The lack of such an image and Christianity's failure in that respect prompt much of Sherrard's thinking across his later years, his search for a humanity that escapes the dualisms of body and spirit, of God and creation.

II

That opposition to dualism emerges in a different but not unrelated realm in Sherrard's next book, *Church, Papacy, and Schism*. In 1959, in the fourth chapter of *The Greek East and the Latin West*, he had already set out his understanding of the nature

---

15. *Christianity and Eros*, p. 48.

of the Christian Church and begun to explore Western ecclesiology as it came to be centred on the papacy.[16] He is suspicious,
even in 1959, of the Church as an imperial institution and of the
corporate papal Church. The 1978 book develops that position,
though now more explicitly in the context of dualism; of which
schism itself might seem to be an example. But as he had argued
in *The Greek East and the Latin West*, there can be no schism within
the Church. He argues that if the Church is understood as 'a simple
building within which men and women gather in order to worship
God', or as 'an institution organized very much along the lines of
any other human institution or society',[17] then division and schism
are entirely possible. But that is a profound misunderstanding of
the Church.

For Sherrard, it is not a society of common belief, like organis-
ations of a social or political kind. It is constituted by its transcendent nature: 'it is both uncreated and created, trans-historical and
historical, simultaneously.'[18] The Church is the point, within time
and space, where the historical opens to the gifts of God: 'God in
the Person of the Holy Spirit is the immanent substantial form of
the Church, the immanent interior principle of its unity and its
ontological realization.'[19] And, because God is always one, never
divided, the Church is also always one by virtue of the unity of the
divine nature that it makes available to humanity.

Schism, then, is real only when the Church has ceased to be
what it really is, the *locus* of the sacramental unity of God with the
human. This union is always personal, from both directions; God is
always known in his persons, and it is human beings as persons
who enter that union:

---

16. 'Sacerdotium and Regnum in the Greek East and the Latin West', *Greek
East and Latin West*, pp. 73–107.
17. *Church, Papacy, Schism*, p. 1.
18. *Church, Papacy, Schism*, p. 3.
19. *Church, Papacy, Schism*, p. 3.

It must be remembered that in Christ it is not one human nature but all human nature that is united to God; and the Church is not merely the body universal of those who share the light of the faith, a *societas hominum fidelium* or *congregatio hominum fidelium* [a gathering of the faithful], but is the *locus* of the continuing theandric mystery, the mystery of the incarnation, in which all human beings are called to participate.[20]

That participation happens on the level of the individual. It is individual persons, not the institution, that participate in the mystery; and that participation is direct, not mediated by the institution. The question is how a Church so understood came to be what Sherrard now sees: an institution divided and alienated from the majority in the modern world.

He answers through a closer definition of the Church. The Church is founded in sacrament; the union of God with humanity is realised in the sacrament of that unity, which is the Eucharist. And that is the Church: 'where Christ is manifest in the Eucharist, there is the Catholic Church. And as Christ is manifest in each local church in which the Eucharist is celebrated, each local church is itself *the* Catholic Church'. It is Catholic not by virtue of geographical extent or institutional affiliation but by its 'expression of the fullness, the completeness or plenitude of the truth which is Christ'.[21]

At the centre of this eucharistic life is the bishop. Christ gave the Eucharist to his apostles, and the apostles, in good order, handed it on to those who succeeded them, who were the bishops. They are what they are because they are the agents of the continuation of Christ's mystery. Their office 'is what it is because through occupying it its holder is entitled to act as the image of Christ in the

---

20. *Church, Papacy, Schism*, p. 4.
21. *Church, Papacy, Schism*, p. 14.

celebration of that eucharistic mystery through which the Church is made manifest on earth'.[22] The bishop is the bearer of the mystery, and so defining of the Church. It is in the person of the bishop that the Church continues the mystery that unites God with the human, and so makes Incarnation real. Just as the Incarnation is an image of participation, so the Church, for Sherrard, is by nature participatory: it makes possible human participation in the divine. It does so materially through the Eucharist, in which material things, bread and wine, participate in Christ.

Yet, this is not the Church that Sherrard finds around him in the West. Somehow this model has been betrayed. The problem, as he understands it, lies in the relationship between the essence of the Church, which is local and eucharistic, and its broader institutional expression. He recognises that the Church must have such an expression. The Church may be 'a theandric, a divine-human reality', but,

> this does not mean ... that the Church has no institutional aspect, no social and human form necessary for its operation on earth, in time and place, in history, and among communities of men and women ... It does not mean that the Church does not have to 'incarnate' itself in specific offices and disciplines responsible for regulating and guiding its activities on earth.[23]

All that is humanly necessary. But in recognising those realities, it has been possible, if not to forget, at least to give a lower place to the Church 'as a eucharistic reality, as the body of Christ'.[24]

This is not, for Sherrard, simply a matter of historical ecclesiology. His understanding of the Eucharist arises from his meta-

---

22. *Church, Papacy, Schism*, p. 18.
23. *Church, Papacy, Schism*, p. 39.
24 Ibid.

physics. The material world, the world of time and space available to our senses, participates in another reality. Seen in this way

> the material, the created or the phenomenal is seen not as constituting a reality in its own right, set apart from and as it were parallel, but on a lower level, to the spiritual, the uncreated, or the noumenal. Visible is related to invisible, or material to spiritual, not so much as effect is to extrinsic cause, but more as being the mode in which the invisible or the spiritual exists in time and space.[25]

There are few passages more important for Sherrard's metaphysics. He is arguing for a co-inherence of the material and the spiritual; and in so doing he is rejecting the dualism of 'created' and 'uncreated' and of 'above' and 'below'. He is rejecting the dualism of the divine as cause and the material world as effect. But he is also rejecting the dualism of the contemporary West, where the material world, the object of science, is one thing, and the spiritual world, if it has any reality, is something else. He is insisting on a unity: the materiality which we inhabit and are *is* the spiritual, in the mode that is available to us.

The conception of the Church that came to dominate the West relied on a quite different metaphysics. Sherrard had argued in *The Greek East and the Latin West* that medieval Latin theology, and particularly the Aristotelian theology of Aquinas, distinguished between two modes of knowledge, revelation and reason. One effect of that division was that the material world, the world open to reason, came to constitute a distinct and self-contained reality. Its nature and working were increasingly explained by the operation of reason, and so it had no need of God. After that change, the world is seen differently:

---

25. *Church, Papacy, Schism*, p. 40.

The visible world is one of natures and causes, potentialities and actions, not a symbolic world showing forth the divine, not an epiphany or a theophany. In other words, the sense of the participation – of the created in the uncreated, the material in the spiritual – is less effective. Visible things are seen not as participating in, still less as modes of existence of, invisible realities.[26]

The bond of participation has been broken. For Aquinas and those who followed him, the only instrument left to establish a connection between visible and invisible was analogy: human love might be an analogy of God's love. That might aid human understanding, but the gulf between the two loves was still absolute.

In the West, God and the world gradually pull apart; the material world, offering its richness to rational discovery, becomes the real object of interest. At the same time a division opens in the way that the Church is understood. In the belief that Christ is the eternal High Priest and that the faithful are gathered in heaven, doctrine teaches that there is an invisible and heavenly Church, the Church Triumphant. But immediately and historically there is the Church on earth, the Church Militant. That is the Church that humanity can know, the institution with its doctrine and hierarchy; and that becomes the reality of the Church for the world. There are, for the faithful, two Churches, and their interpenetration is weakened. A dualism emerges. The earthly Church is separated from its transcendental reality, is freed as an institution to manage itself with the priorities and methods of the world.

Out of a local gathering around the mystery, Sherrard traces the growth of a corporate and authoritarian Church. With the conversion of the empire, the structure of the Church came to be modelled on the structure of the empire; the word 'diocese' originally signified

---

26. *Church, Papacy, Schism*, p. 41.

a civil unit of the empire. The Church, now the religion of all citizens, needed governance; and there was a model to hand. The pressure to adopt that model intensified as the civil power of the empire declined, and as the Church became, in effect, the replacing authority, the only institution that could still claim universality across the Roman world.

To do that it needed a centre of authority; and the see of Rome, the ancient imperial capital and the place of the martyrdoms of Peter and Paul, was best placed to claim that position against its rivals in Jerusalem, Antioch and Alexandria. With the elevation of the Roman see to primacy, the monarchical structure of the Church was confirmed. Just as Augustus as *princeps* had 'possessed the highest authority in the state', had 'represented the principle of primacy',[27] so the Bishop of Rome ceased to be a bishop among bishops and acquired a quasi-imperial status. The papacy understood itself in those terms as a 'principate'; and it used Christ's commission, '*tu es Petrus*', to justify that position.[28] But Sherrard suspects that the process was the other way round:

> It might be suggested that the fact that the Church on earth came to be regarded as a juristic, corporate, and governable body of Christians demanding to be ruled on a monarchical basis, and the fact that the model for this monarchy was found in the Roman Principate, forced on the Roman church and its advisers that particular interpretation of the Petrine commission and its consequences which is maintained down to the present day.[29]

It was the principate that determined the reading, not the reading that justified the principate. The pope became, in his person as

---

27. *Church, Papacy, Schism*, p. 56.
28. Matthew 16:18.
29. *Church, Papacy, Schism*, pp. 56–7.

successor of Peter, the final authority in a hierarchical, corporate Church. And as the Vicar of Christ his authority was a transcendental authority; the Church so organised controlled human access to the divine.

It would be hard to conceive of anything further from Sherrard's understanding of the Church. The mystery of the Eucharist was still there in the Roman Church; the Mass was its daily practice. But the decisive moment for individual salvation was entry into that incorporation of belief that was the Church. The body of Christ was no longer the eucharistic body; it became the institution, the corporate body of the Church, which in its institutional existence was Christ's presence on earth. Sherrard summarises:

> Incorporation into this mystical body, therefore, is not alone or even above all through participation in the Eucharist. It is also – and in effect primarily – through membership of the visible institutional form of the Church and subscription to its laws. ... One cannot share in the catholicity of the Church of Christ or be a member of the body of Christ without this membership and subscription to the visible institution of the Church.[30]

The local church is Church by virtue of its incorporation in the institution, not, as Sherrard understand it, by its celebration of the mystery. Local churches become, if not franchises of the institution, at least *filiales*, branches, authenticated by their formal relation to the institution to which they belong.

Sherrard has identified two dualisms in the history of the Western Church – an epistemological dualism between revelation and reason, and an ecclesiological dualism between the Church in heaven and the institutional gatekeeper, the Church on earth. From

---

30. *Church, Papacy, Schism*, p. 47.

those disjunctions flows a third, one that has affected the life of the West, cultural as well as intellectual. Because the Church presents itself as agent and proprietor of the spiritual, all that has to do with the divine comes to be seen as the business of the Church; it becomes a separate zone, professionalised, distinct from the general life of the community. The Church comes to be seen as the embassy of another world, an extra-territoriality of heaven, rather than the epiphany of what already is. Instead of participating in the materiality of the human, it offers an alternative, spiritualised and accessible only through its doors. Explicitly or implicitly, Catholic or Protestant, it calls for the world to be rejected. It places in doubt the validity in human terms of human existence.

At the same time, Sherrard suggests, the Church begins to view itself differently. Although it still affirms its transcendental nature, the institutional Church is itself vulnerable to the exclusive identification of transcendence with revelation, which is God's affair. The Church is left with the world, and its first reality comes to be its life within history; increasingly, it understands itself through earthly purposes and ends. These may be bad or good: the conversion of the heathen, the creation of a just society. But Sherrard questions whether the Church exists to fulfil any function beyond itself. The Church, for him, is not an instrument to any end; it is what it is always and already, the locus and epiphany of Incarnation. The Church 'is its own end or purpose; and to use it or regard it as a means to achieve some collective purpose – however noble or Christian it may appear – is to cut it off from its living roots in the Person of Christ.'[31] The Church is not to be incorporated into the projects of humanity, any more than it was to be defined by structures inherited from the Roman Empire. For Sherrard, the mistake is the same in both cases – the failure to see the Church as mystery, as the point of Incarnation at the heart of all that humanity does.

---

31. *Church, Papacy, Schism*, p. 28.

In the later part of *Church, Papacy, and Schism*, Sherrard explores the eleventh-century schism in detail, in relation to Christology and to Trinitarian theology. The first four chapters of the book, though, are what convey the essence of Sherrard's argument and the intensity of his opposition to dualism. He points to where the faults lie: the failure of the Church properly to understand its participation in the divine, and the consequent failure of an increasingly rationalist world to see its participation in a transcendent reality.

To show how participation can overcome the real distinctions of human experience – male and female, earthly and heavenly – requires an argument that Sherrard does not yet have. For the moment he has a blunt solution, namely to assert that, contrary to appearance, everything is one. He is too aware of the reality of difference, of the creative productivity of individuality, to see all distinctions swallowed in a simplistic monism. There needs to be a logic that does not make of difference and unity another, and more basic, dualism.

III

These two books of the 1970s contain some of Sherrard's most direct statements of his own faith. What is striking is how completely he appears to accept the traditional language, as, for example, in this passage from *Church, Papacy, and Schism*:

> The incarnation – the Logos made flesh, made man – because it takes place in the actuality of the fallen world means that God has to veil the glory of his divinity in such a way that it becomes accessible to man's lack of spiritual vision, to his opacity and blindness, and so can be received and assimilated by man.[32]

---

32. *Church, Papacy, Schism*, pp. 5–6.

He is speaking of the necessary materiality of divine revelation for the material beings we are. The language is the conventional language of faith, and the idea itself is conventional, reflected in many English hymns. Nor are the terms qualified: there was a Fall, there was an Incarnation. Sherrard emerges as orthodox as well as Orthodox. It is left to the reader to know what to make of this, in relation to his generally less conventional thinking.

Again it must be remembered how central myth is for Sherrard. As early as 1956, in *The Marble Threshing Floor*, he made this very inclusive statement:

> Myth is the natural language of the supra-individual world. Only in terms of those symbols and images that constitute a myth is it possible to give expression, not to that which is transient, but to that which abides through all change. Only in those terms can the inner reality of man's life be mirrored.[33]

Myth is humanly necessary. An assumption of contemporary culture, however, is that what is said in myth might be said in some other way, might be said more accurately – that myth is a colourful but incompetent way of handling truth. Sherrard's point is that, for the kind of truth in prospect, myth is its language. No excuse is required for inhabiting that language, for using it to do the work that only it can do. The truth of the Fall is not that of a historic event, but of the relation between the being that humanity has and its intuition of what it might have been.

So, to use conventional Christian language is to inhabit the myth, not as falling short of conceptual language but as the only language available. Yet, the frame of myth is expansive. How closely he relates Christianity to myth in general, and to the mythic mysteries of the ancient world, can be seen in these words, again of

---

33. *Marble Threshing*, p. 235.

1956: 'In the Christian myth of Byzantine Greece were enshrined in the main the same principles as those of the Orphic and Pythagorean tradition. Only the moral bias of Christianity, the intrusion into its mythology of a dualistic ethic ... divided the two traditions.'[34] Myth is the essence, a continuous thread. But when a faith comes to understand itself primarily in ethical terms, the unity of myth breaks down, and dualism once again triumphs.

If Sherrard's language is often conventionally orthodox, his thinking is not. For a Christianity that stresses its historical nature, he offers, without apology, myth. For Christianity that in its Western forms has placed morality at the centre, he proposes ethicism as an intrusion, a distortion. Sherrard is also unconventional in his placing of Christianity alongside other faiths. With the Christian vocabulary there is a universalism; myths, though various, do not exclude each other. Sherrard recognised that in 1956 in his discussion of Dionysios Solomos in *The Marble Threshing Floor*. In his poem about the Greek War of Independence, 'The Free Besieged', Solomos creates his own myth:

> The whole action of the poem, from start to finish, unfolds as it were within the omnipresence of the Great Mother and receives its significance by participation in a drama that is above all her drama. For she, a divine power and the source of man's life, dwells, as Solomos puts it in 'The Cretan', where she can see 'into the abyss and into the heart of man'.[35]

Later, Sherrard draws the Christian parallel:

> We can only find a parallel to this in the imaginative pattern of Solomos'[s] poetry if we are prepared to recognise in Mary

---

34. *Marble Threshing*, pp. 235–6.
35. *Marble Threshing*, p. 28.

a symbol of an eternal feminine, of a 'donna-Divinità', Sophia, whose celestial ray or Word lies concealed in a darkness enveloped by greater darkness; and if, further, we are prepared to equate this ray or Word with the spiritual consciousness that man possesses 'in the beginning'.[36]

Mary is Solomos's Great Mother, the eternal feminine, the female Wisdom of the Hebrew scriptures. Myths echo and reinforce each other. In the significance that Solomos gives to sacrifice, Sherrard sees a parallel to Christ's passion:

> Although the cross as such, or any specific symbol which may be said to replace it, does not appear in Solomos'[s] poetry, 'The Free Besieged' does nevertheless represent much the same action as that which Christ performed through his passion: the freeing of man from all the ties that bind him to his ordinary and imprisoned self.[37]

If myths can parallel each other, if they can point to a common truth, there is no basis for a Church that claims sole access. Myth establishes a human commonality.

Myth is a way of knowing, and like all ways of knowing, it can be in error. As early as the 1950 lecture on El Greco, Sherrard points to what he takes to be an inadequacy in the myths of the Upanishads and the Gnostics.[38] Yet, myth remains for him central to the human capacity for understanding, a common ground of the human spirit. Out of that common ground grows his openness to other religions, there in some words from one of his last essays. If Christ is the epiphany of the Logos in the human sphere, it is also true that 'any deep reading of another religion is a reading of the Logos, of Christ.

---

36. *Marble Threshing*, p. 246.
37. *Marble Threshing*, p. 247.
38. *Blood and Light* 186–7.

It is the Logos who is received in the spiritual illumination of a Brahmin, a Buddhist, or a Moslem.'[39] Nor are the routes to that illumination necessarily different. One is contemplation, which for Sherrard is at the centre of all spirituality. Athos had shown him that, but Christianity has no monopoly. Writing to George Seferis in March 1950, he says of ancient Greece, 'I sometimes wonder whether Heraklitos and Plato were not, if not mystics, at least contemplatives, having experiences which their writings grope to express.'[40]

IV

Non-Christian spiritualities of a different kind engage Sherrard's sympathy in his 1975 essay on W. B. Yeats. He follows Yeats's life as a spiritual journey, as a sequence of false starts and new beginnings, but the object throughout is the overcoming of dualism and the achieving of a unifying vision.

Once again, mythology is at the centre. Yeats, he says, aspired to belong to the line of the greatest poets, of Homer, Dante, Milton and Goethe; and 'he recognized consequently that there can be no great poetry that is not rooted in a mythology and no mythology that is not rooted in metaphysical tradition. Great poetry is the poetry of the great theme and this theme is metaphysical.'[41] Myth, for Sherrard, is the language and materialisation of metaphysics, whether Plato's myth of the forms or the Irish myth of the Danaan; it is the language through which the metaphysical enters human lives. Modern culture has made the mistake of believing that human beings can step outside myth that, just as we might abandon metaphysics, myth is a thing of the past.

---

39. In 'Christianity and Other Sacred Traditions'; chapter 3 of Philip Sherrard, *Christianity: Lineaments of a Sacred Tradition* (Brookline, MA: Holy Cross Orthodox Press, 1998), p. 62.
40. *Blood and Light*, p. 131.
41. *Yeats*, p. 3.

Sherrard admires Yeats for not making that mistake. From his earliest poetry, myth was the language of his sensibility and the source of that myth was tradition. There was the Christian tradition, but 'that was not the only tradition in Ireland'. 'Underlying Christian Ireland was the tradition of pre-Christian Ireland – the Ireland of the Tuatha De Danaan and the *sidhe*, of Oisin, and Niamh and Aengus. This was a tradition older than that of any European Church, and founded upon the experience of the world before the modern bias.'[42] This was more than a reservoir of tales: it was a way of knowing the world. For Yeats, to enter the realm of myth was to acquire a 'gnosis': by studying the tradition he 'thought he might rediscover a symbolical language reaching far back into the past and expressing the spiritual values of his country before the English conquest and the still more devastating invasions of the modern scientific mentality'.[43]

Sherrard finds in Yeats an ally. He is sympathetic to Yeats's search for a key to the meaning of mythologies, for some frame that will elucidate, not just Irish myth, but all myth. Yeats turned to theosophy, and Sherrard can see why: its teachings were a corrective to the prevailing cultural assumptions. They allowed Yeats to think of 'cyclic theories of time', those cycles 'varying in length, of death and rebirth, alternatively lunar and solar, sub-jective and objective, imaginative and rational, through which individual life and the life of civilizations pass'.[44] Like Sherrard, Yeats cast his net wide: besides Madame Blavatsky there were Blake, Böhme, Swedenborg, Plato and Plotinus. But he does not share every step of Yeats's path. Sherrard suggests that Yeats lacked any structure of spiritual practice within which those teachings might have become inward and personal. 'There is little or no point in knowing about metaphysical matters or the eternal

42. *Yeats*, p. 5.
43. *Yeats*, p. 6.
44. *Yeats*, pp. 7–8.

verities on the abstract level'. They must be vivified 'in one's own consciousness and actions'.[45]

One attempted solution for Yeats was magic, the Kabbalah and Rosicrucianism, the esotericism of 'A Vision'. But for Sherrard that forced him unavoidably into dualism:

> Magic is essentially dualistic. It demands, not a participation in the created reality of things, but the exercise of a superior mental force set over against and separated from this reality. In simple terms, the dualism is one of mind and matter, and from this point of view the practice of magic represents a process of abstraction. It involves an increasing withdrawal from the world of time and place, a progressive devaluation of the world.[46]

But the point for Yeats was exactly that, to move away; magic and vision gave access to his ideal world, his Tír na nÓg, which was 'outside time, outside place, less perhaps because it was a metaphysical world than because it lay remotely, irrecoverably, in the past'.[47]

Haunted by such dualisms, what was Yeats to do? His struggle is there in the Byzantium poems, heavy with the weariness of human materiality, seeking a reality of formal abstraction, the 'artifice of eternity'.[48] There he imagines himself discarnate, 'out of nature', where the perfection of a moonlit dome disdains 'all that man is'.[49] The failing body and the turmoil of mind and feeling are to be rejected; yet the rejection is impossible because the world cannot be rejected, and the dualism remains.

---

45. *Yeats*, p. 9.
46. *Yeats*, p. 12.
47. Ibid.
48. W. B. Yeats, 'Sailing to Byzantium', in *The Tower* (London: Renard Press, 1928), and 'Byzantium', in *The Winding Stair and Other Poems* (London: Simon & Schuster, 1933).
49. *Yeats*, p. 15.

In his last years, Sherrard suggests, Yeats moved away from this abstract and essentially Platonic ideal of perfection. His path lay partly through the pre-Socratic philosophers and the Orphic mystery, with its claim to transform body and mind. Towards the end, in the middle and late 1930s, it was the teaching of Hinduism that brought him relief:

> It was ... with the help of the Hindu tradition that in his final years Yeats was able to free his thought from the last traces of its dualism and to achieve the unity for which he had sought so long. It was a unity that set him free to speak out of the fullness of himself, out of his own nature ... to see everything, from the heroic figures of Irish legend and history down to 'a mound of refuse or the sweepings of the street' as part of the great sacred drama, the great sacred dance.[50]

'To see everything': the vision had found space for the 'foul rag-and-bone shop of the heart'.[51]

Yeats, like Blake before him, provided Sherrard with an example of the unifying vision. But his struggle with dualism is not over; the conflict continues through his later works, whether in addressing the dualism of humanity and nature in *The Rape of Man and Nature* or that of form and materiality in *The Sacred in Life and Art*. Nevertheless, it is at its most intense in these writings of the 1970s. Insofar as the problem has a solution, it lies always in participation, the participation of body with spirit in sexuality, the participation of earth with heaven in a true understanding of the Church. Nor is this an abstract philosophical problem. In his discussion of Yeats he shows how the conflicts of dualism can

---

50. *Yeats*, p. 17.
51. W. B. Yeats, 'The Circus Animals' Desertion', in *Last Poems and Two Plays* (Dublin: Cuala Press, 1939).

shape a life, personally and creatively. When some unifying vision is achieved, the world is transformed; something emerges that dualism had concealed, and to that Sherrard gives the name 'the sacred'.

PART II
The Human Image

5

Persons and Participation

A reader of Philip Sherrard is likely to notice that, sometime around the mid-1970s, a change takes place. His earlier writings, from the letters and essays of the 1940s to the short books of the 1970s, are concerned with specific subjects, chiefly ecclesiological or Greek; whereas his later writings take on broader issues, move to a wider and more ambitious scale. At the same time the tone of his writing changes. It becomes more polemical; there is the sense of a man fighting a cause, no longer satisfied with analysis and interpretation. The aims and methods of 'modern science' often come under explicit attack.

There is much anger in this later work. Sherrard feels intensely about a time in which humanity is increasingly atrophied, and the world placed in jeopardy. Under that intensity of feeling his manner can be provocative. He will sometimes assert rather than argue, dismiss contrary positions, stylistically insert an 'of course' where it is hardly a matter of 'of course'.

It is important in reading these later books to look beneath the occasional distractions of manner to what is being said; the same mind is at work, fed by the same enormously inclusive reading that crosses the boundaries of usual expectation. Many of Sherrard's earlier themes remain the same; they do so, however, within a frame less cultural and historical and more cosmological. One reflection of this is that Sherrard writes directly about nature and humanity's place in nature. He asks questions about what it is that we inhabit. This movement towards a totality of understanding is part of his search for a unifying vision. If we are to know the universe and ourselves, we must see the whole.

I

Although not published until 1987, most of *The Rape of Man and Nature* dates from the 1970s, and chiefly from lectures given at King's College, London, in 1975.[1] The central text, though, is the fourth chapter of the book, 'The Desanctification of Nature'. This was originally an independent article, written two years earlier in 1973.[2] As its title suggests, it raises the question of the sacred, of how that word might still be applied to the natural world and, by extension, to humanity. For Sherrard, the loss of the word in contemporary discourse had its source in the dualism of the Western mind that he traced from the thirteenth century. With the separation of the realms of revelation and reason, and with the emergence of an autonomous area of empirically-derived knowledge that had no dependence on the transcendent, a word like 'sacred' was no longer needed. Inasmuch as the word was still used, it referred to special places and objects, made special by human perceptions of them: a sacred book, a sacred mountain.

How that came about is suggested in the subtitle to the book: *An Enquiry into the Origins and Consequences of Modern Science*. It is science that has desacralized our image of the world by

---

1. Philip Sherrard, *The Rape of Man and Nature: An Enquiry into the Origins and Consequences of Modern Science* (Ipswich: Golgonooza Press, 1987). Chapters 1, 2 and 3 were the Frederick Denison Maurice lectures of October 1975 at King's College London, where Sherrard was lecturer in the History of the Orthodox Church. Referred to subsequently as *Rape of Man*.
2. Originally published in Derek Baker (ed.) *Studies in Church History*, vol. 10 (Oxford: Basil Blackwell, 1973).

establishing a discourse in which the word 'sacred' can have no place. Even if it had been the intention to speak of the sacred, even if the sacred emerged in experience, the dominant language disallowed it.

This exclusion of the sacred was not just a matter for secular society: it had its impact on the mind of the Western Church, on its understanding of the relationship between God and creation. To state the issue in that way immediately reveals the difficulty: on the one hand God, on the other the world. Sherrard has no confidence that the matter can be addressed in such dualistic terms, but they are the terms embedded in the Christian mind of the West:

> There has been a growing tendency within the post-mediaeval Christian world to look upon creation as the artefact of a Maker who as it were has produced it from without. This has provided us with a picture of a God in heaven who, having set the cosmic process in motion and having left it to run more or less on its own according to its own laws, now interferes directly on but rare occasions and then only in the form of special and 'abnormal' acts operated upon the world from without.[3]

Apart from the general implausibility of this model, Sherrard is keen to stress the externality that it implies: God stands apart, separated from creation by an unpassable ontological gulf.

Yet Sherrard must accept that God's being is not our being. His task is to respect that, without reducing God to the being of the world or reinforcing the prevailing dualism of creator and created. His starting-point is the Incarnation. If that is taken seriously – and Sherrard suspects that in Western circles it often is not – then the divine and the human become one, 'without confusion, without

---

3. *Rape of Man*, p. 91.

change, without division, without separation'.[4] Christ is one person: his divinity is human, his humanity is divine. The two, both present, can be distinguished but not separated. There is no dualism. And insofar as Christ is present in the Eucharist, the same is true:

> The material sign of the sacrament is not simply something to which the Spirit is attached, as if the Spirit were an extraneous element added to the matter, or one that 'transubstantiates' the matter through his presence. On the contrary, they [the Greek Fathers] insist that there is a total integration of the material and the spiritual, so that the elements of bread and wine are an actual mode of existence of the divine and there is a complete union between them.[5]

Sherrard's target is any form of externality; he is following the Greek Fathers in insisting on 'a total integration'. On such a possibility depends, besides belief in the Incarnation and the Eucharist, any sense of nature as sacred or of humanity participating in any reality beyond its own material and temporal being.

Sherrard sees the Latin doctrine of transubstantiation as revealing the opening gulf in the West. Since the material world is (following the Scholastics) its own realm and (following Augustine) fallen and corrupt, the only way in which God can be present within it is to do something to it: in effect, to intrude upon it. There is no intrinsic presence; there is only grace operating from outside. All that can be claimed for nature is that it retains the capacity to receive that grace. But the divine does not work *ab extra*. For Sherrard, all externality is bound to create dualism: there is one thing working on another, God on nature, grace on humanity. But a proper understanding of sacrament says otherwise. 'Sacrament presupposes an actual incar-

---

4. The formula of the Council of Chalcedon, 451, on Christ's two natures.
5. *Rape of Man*, p. 93.

nation of divine power and life');[6] it recognises a unity of the material and the divine. To see the world in that way

> means that nature is regarded not as something upon which God acts from without. It is regarded as something through which God expresses Himself from within. Nature, or creation ... is perceived as the self-expression of the divine, and the divine is totally present within it. ... In creating what is created, it is Himself that God creates, in another mode. In creation He becomes His own image.[7]

This act of self-expression, Sherrard argues, is not a decision that God might or might not have made towards something external to himself, pre-existing 'matter' or 'nothingness'; it is to be understood as the realisation of what God is *in himself*:

> The created world is God's sacrament of Himself to Himself in His creatures; it is the means whereby He is what He is. Were there no creation, then God would be other than He is; and if creation were not sacramental, then God would not be its creator and there would be no question of a sacrament anywhere. If God is not present in a grain of sand then He is not present in heaven either.[8]

Creation, for Sherrard, is implicit in the being of God. It is *how* he is *what* he is.

Sherrard's image of the creator-created relationship is remarkably intimate. Creation is in the very being of God; and it is in creation that he comes to himself. There is no dualism. But

---

6. *Rape of Man*, p. 93.
7. Ibid.
8. Ibid. 'In a grain of sand' echoes the first line of Blake's poem, 'Auguries of Innocence'.

duality is preserved; there is God, there is the world. Both are real; neither is a shadow or extrapolation of the other. But neither is external to the other; the being of the one is inextricable from the being of the other, always in a mutuality of realisation. Creation cannot exist without the creator, but the creator cannot be what he is without creation.

II

It is the loss of such an image of mutuality that underlies, for Sherrard, the desacralisation of the modern world. This theme is developed in the Maurice lectures. In the 1973 article, Sherrard's concern had been with the loss of the sacred in nature; in the lectures he is concerned with the desacralisation of the human, which he also sees as a dehumanisation.

The first of the King's College lectures, 'The Human Image', explores the prevailing images of the human in the history of the West. There is, first, the image of the human generated by the Reformers of the sixteenth century from their reading of the Hebrew scriptures. In this view,

> God absolutely transcends man; there is an absolute separate-
> ness and heterogeneity between them; and man sees himself
> as an insignificant creature whose life can achieve positive
> content only on condition that he submits himself without
> reserve to the autocratic, unlimited and overwhelming
> majesty that rules the world and that issues appropriate com-
> mands for its good governance.[9]

This implies that 'God and man constitute two distinct ontological realities, and between them there is no real kinship or inner

---

9. *Rape of Man*, p. 20.

identity'.[10] This model took its justification, Sherrard suggests, from the father of Western theology, Augustine. For him, '[man] is merely the slave of the congenital principle of sin, the depraved creature of a transcendent God whose nature is totally other than his own and who may, through filling man's emptiness with an external gift of grace, save him from damnation if He so wills.'[11] Once again, Sherrard shows himself hostile to externality. For Augustine salvation came through grace; but 'grace ... is not something extrinsic, not something added to man's nature; it is inherent in the conditions of his birth.'[12]

A view such as that of the Reformers, with its determination to preserve the absolute transcendence of God, has the effect not just of alienating the human in its fallen nature, but also of making Incarnation impossible: between the two natures, divine and human, there can only be an absolute difference. The humanity that Augustine characterised – fallen, captive to a fallen creation – could never have been one with the divine. From that grew a false understanding of Incarnation, as itself a unique action *ab extra*. The result has been a tendency in the West to see Christ predominantly in terms of one or the other nature, rather than as a person in which the two natures join. See him solely in terms of the divine and Christ becomes 'a kind of unique exception', 'someone so essentially different from us that He cannot serve as a model of what we ourselves have it in us to become'.[13] See him as solely human and Christ is close to God because he was a very good man. Both views fail to see the unity; neither grasp what is involved in Incarnation.

Sherrard's response is to return to Plato. Again, the key is participation. Plato's forms, the ideas or archetypes that shape all material existents, stand in a participatory relation to those existents. As far

---

10. *Rape of Man*, p. 20.
11. *Rape of Man*, p. 22.
12. Ibid.
13. *Rape of Man*, p. 19.

as those existents are intelligible, it is because they share the intelligibility of the archetypes:

> Such a conception of the immanence of the transcendent archetype in its sensible counterpart, or of the indwelling of the sensible form in its intelligible archetype, is expressed in terms of the participation of the one in the other. ... In some sense, the image is the archetype in another mode, and only differs from the archetype because the conditions in which it is manifested impose on it a different form.[14]

There is no uncrossable ontological gulf between the archetypes and the material world of the kind that Augustinian theology promotes. Plato's universe 'is this structure of participation which constitutes the great golden chain of being'. 'In this structure there is nothing that is not animate, nothing that is mere dead matter. All is endowed with being, all – even the least particle – belongs to a living transmuting whole. Each thing is the revelation of the indwelling creative spirit.'[15] It was this philosophical context, Sherrard argues, that enabled the early Greek Fathers to give an account of the Incarnation. Just as Platonism showed how material things could participate in the non-material, so they could conceive of the material Christ as participating in the being of God.

Sherrard goes on to trace how this participatory frame was lost in the West. There was Augustine's interpretation of the Fall, of a gulf between God and the human that could be breached only from God's side. But there was also the Aristotelian revolution in Western theology in the thirteenth century. One effect of that was the loss of any sense of the participation of the material world in a reality beyond itself. Because Aristotle denied what Plato affirmed, there

---

14. *Rape of Man*, p. 23–4.
15. *Rape of Man*, p. 24.

was nothing transcendent for the material to participate in. Further, because of his insistence on the absolute particularity of substances, no two entities could share a substance. That made the doctrine of transubstantiation necessary. But it also effectively negated Incarnation.

The theological consequences of the new Aristotelianism were serious. But the loss went beyond the Church and the theology of the person of Christ; it began to govern the general image of the human. If it became hard to see how Christ could embody God in man, it became even harder to see how that might be true of every human being. Sherrard is insistent: the Incarnation is not an exception. It is the revelation of our own nature. Lose the ability to make sense of it and we lose the ability to understand ourselves.

Plato provided a model of the participation of different modes of being, but Sherrard still needs to give his own account of that participation. He does so through the word *perichoresis*, a word that appears for the first time in *The Rape of Man and Nature*. The Greek word, as a noun, does not appear in classical literary texts, though there is a verb, *perichoreo*, which means 'to move or circle around'. The etymology may have to do with dance. Sherrard's source for the word is the Greek Fathers, who use it to discuss the relationship between the persons of the Trinity.[16]

Sherrard uses *perichoresis* to speak of a mode of being that is not just participatory but also reciprocal:

> The word which perhaps most fully conveys the degree of reciprocity involved in the idea of Christ's divine humanity is the Greek word *perichoresis* – a word which expresses the

---

16. The word appears as a noun first in the writing of St Maximus the Confessor (seventh century), but the verb had appeared earlier in the work of Gregory of Nazianzus (fourth century). The noun does appear in modern Greek, where it has the sense of interpenetration.

dynamic co-penetration of the uncreated and the created, the divine and the human, and so something more than is implied by the phrase, *communicatio idiomatum*, with which it is sometimes equated.[17]

The Latin phrase, which attempts to speak of what is shared between the divine and human natures of Christ, helps by contrast to clarify Sherrard's position. In the *communicatio* there is a transfer of properties: the divine nature takes on some of the properties of the human (such as the ability to suffer), the human takes on some of the properties of the divine (such as to be without sin). Insofar as there is a sharing, though, it is only of properties, not of nature. Sherrard's *perichoresis* involves more than that: full co-penetration or coinherence. He has in view a mode of being in which two natures join, without ceasing to be distinct. In the first chapter of his next book, *The Sacred in Life and Art*, he illustrates *perichoresis* through the example of marriage:

> It is as in the sacrament of marriage in which the beloved otherness of the two partners itself constitutes the matter or ground of the sacrament: *finis amoris ut duo unam fiant.*[18] It is not a case of the complete absorption of the one in the other. … But each finds its own identity in the other.[19]

The Incarnation was a *perichoresis* of the divine and the human: neither nature was lost, both were joined in a single person. This was not a sharing or exchange of properties. A transaction in which God made himself humanly vulnerable or a man became

---

17. *Rape of Man*, p. 25–6. The Latin phrase, literally 'communication of properties', may be as old as Ignatius of Antioch (*c*.100) but was ratified by the First Council of Ephesus in 431.
18. 'The goal of love is that two should be one'.
19. *Sacred in Life*, p. 7.

divinely compassionate would not have been Incarnation. In Incarnation the two natures co-inhere without ceasing to be what they are.

The power of *perichoresis* for Sherrard is that it preserves duality without creating a dualism. There is the divine and there is the human, and both are real and distinguishable. Yet they are not in opposition: each makes the other what it is. Sherrard argues that God would not be God without becoming human, just as the human is not human without God as its goal. As the existence of the material world fulfils a potentiality within the being of God, so God fulfils the potentiality of his own nature by becoming human:

> The divine can only fulfil this potentiality in union with the human, just as the human can only fulfil it in union with the divine. The union of the two natures in Christ is therefore based on a certain inherent polarity between the divine and the human. God and man are in some sense exemplars or paradigms of one another. ... The humanization of God and the deification of man condition each other mutually, for the simple reason that they express a tendency inherent in the nature of each.[20]

Polarity is implicit in *perichoresis*, and it maintains difference: God is not dissolved into man, nor man into God. Between the poles there is interaction, a mutual actualisation, but no opposition.

This Patristic concept helps to solve some of Sherrard's philosophical problems. He recognises in his later writing that Plato can be a source of dualism as much as its resolution. Yes, he constructs a 'golden chain' of interpenetrating being, from the Forms to material entities. But there will always be a tendency within Platonism to see the Forms, the archetypes, as the truly real; to see

---

20. *Rape of Man*, p. 25.

their material derivations as less intelligible and so less real. *Perichoresis* works to preserve both the reality of particulars and of what Plato would have called the archetypes: neither collapses into the other.

Sherrard's aim has been to give a proper account of the Incarnation. *Perichoresis* works for him in resolving the question implicit in the title of the first chapter of this book, 'The Human Image'. The image he is looking for is an image of *perichoresis*: humanity exists in that mode of duality-without-dualism, and its existence in that mode *is* its humanity. The 'dehumanization of man', the title of Sherrard's third chapter, is the loss of that awareness of shared being. It is that which is desacralisation. It is clear that Sherrard's understanding of the word 'sacred' is intimately connected with *perichoresis*. Nature is sacred because it exists in a perichoretic relation with the transcendent; the human is sacred because it exists in a perichoretic relation with the divine. To speak of the sacred is not to set something apart in a holy realm: rather, it is to speak of a unity. For something like *perichoresis* to be real is a precondition both for the sacred and for any unifying vision.

III

His exploration of the Incarnation has led Sherrard to speak of the relation between God and the human, But there is an inward relation that remains to be explored. What is it for the human to be human? What is it to be a person?

Sherrard's answer involves a negotiation between two words, 'person' and 'subject'. His understanding of 'person' is grounded in his theology of the Trinity; it is because personhood is the primary constituent of the divine that we can be persons. 'Subject' points less to the transcendental dimension, more to how we are in the world; it is in contrast with 'object'. 'Subjects' are capable of mutuality, of the relationship that is perichoresis. 'Objects' may interact, but only externally: they cannot share their being. In human experi-ence, our most basic recognition is that we are 'subjects' and 'persons'.

The contemporary world, in particular modern science, gives a different answer. There we know what we are by becoming objects: physical, biological, psychological or social, but always objects, to be measured and counted. As Sherrard puts it, to understand what it is to be human is, for the contemporary world, to look at whatever 'falls within the sphere of physical, biological, psychological or sociological explanation or cognizance'.[21] He does not deny such a sphere, but for him it does no more than reflect the structure of the dominant epistemology: we gain knowledge through the empirical inspection of objects. There is the knower and the known; and to the knower, the known is always an object. Consequently, we become objects to ourselves.

The two self-knowledges are real: we know ourselves as persons and subjects, and we can reflect on ourselves as objects. I can think of the colour of my skin as a biological fact. The question is how to unify those perceptions, how to escape a dualistic view of what it is to be human.

Sherrard begins by pointing to what he describes as a duality in self-experience. There is the domain of rational self-awareness, the 'everyday empirical self' of day-to-day activity. That can be an object of rational knowledge; I can observe my particular purposes and attachments. On that level I can indeed be an object to myself as well as to others, but I am aware of something else:

> I am also aware that there is something in me ... something that surpasses or lies beneath, that level of consciousness with which I normally identify myself – my rational self-consciousness; and I am also aware that this something – of which in fact most of the time I may not be aware – is the real

---

21. *Rape of Man*, p. 16.

centre of my being, is my real self, and that I am not the I of my superficial self-consciousness.[22]

It is there that full self-awareness arises. To know oneself 'is not to know and describe a given or objective reality'; beneath that level of empirical self-knowledge there is an awareness of

something which is the ground of [man's] created nature and which yet cannot be completely identified with this nature: a kind of spiritual subject that gives a wholeness and a stability to his existence and is at the same time his own self at that point at which it is most genuine, creative and unique.[23]

For the Greek Fathers this 'something', this 'spiritual subject', 'if it is not divine, is yet not un-divine'; and Sherrard elaborates:

If it is a potentiality of man's nature to attain divinization – and this is central to the Christian understanding of man here envisaged – there must be in him that which is capable of apprehending the divine and penetrating into it. There must be in him a point of unity between his spirit and the spirit of God: some organ on the borders, so to speak, of the created and the uncreated which is capable of linking both and experiencing both.[24]

The pre-empirical self, the true subject, is this capacity to apprehend and participate in the divine. Sherrard's language here may be less than helpful to his case; to speak of 'some organ' suggests an archaic faculty psychology. The idea, though, has its source in the Greek Fathers, who claim for human beings 'a supra-rational

22. *Rape of Man*, p. 30.
23. *Rape of Man*, p. 31.
24. *Rape of Man*, p. 32.

capacity for knowing and experiencing, a spiritual intellect as distinct from the natural reason' that 'does not form or derive its ideas from material which is external to itself but receives them from an internal fusion with the divine Logos Himself'.[25] What Sherrard is positing is not some area of the brain capable of supernatural knowledge; he is saying that the human capacity for knowing goes beyond object and fact, that it enters a perichoretic relation with ultimate meaning, what Christianity has called the Logos.

It is here, for Sherrard, that the true human subject is to be found. What we know most deeply within ourselves is our capacity for meaning, for participating in the transcendent source of meaning. It is by virtue of that participation that we are subjects and persons. If that is what we are, if personhood is participation, then the unifying vision is what we are intended for, what we already have as we experience ourselves as constituted by this *perichoresis*.

---

25. *Rape of Man*, p. 34.

6

Art and Vision

Philip Sherrard wrote the preface to *The Sacred in Life and Art* in December 1989, two years after the publication of *The Rape of Man and Nature*. Except for one chapter, the book appears to be recent writing. It develops many of the themes of the earlier book, but it does so in a specific area: that of art and the artist.[1]

In the 'Preface' of *The Sacred in Life and Art*, Sherrard strikes a note that becomes more insistent in his later work – one of urgency, even of crisis. Though always engaged with his subjects – Greek poetry and culture, the theology of medieval Europe – there was in his earlier work a degree of academic detachment, something of a view from a distance. Now in the late 1980s that has gone. The attack is direct and personal: contemporary culture has contrived a disaster. As he puts it in the 'Preface',

> the concept of a completely profane world – of a cosmos wholly desacralized – is a fairly recent invention of the human mind, while the endeavour to implement it in practical terms by erecting it into the standard according to which

---

1. Philip Sherrard, *The Sacred in Life and Art* (Ipswich: The Golgonooza Press, 1990). Referred to subsequently as *Sacred in Life*. The exception is chapter 7, 'The Art of Transfiguration', which is based on Sherrard's 1951 Athens lecture on St Symeon the New Theologian (available in its original form in *Blood and Light* 198–208).

we determine the major forms of our social, economic, political and personal life, is still more recent – in fact only now are we becoming aware of the enormity of the self-destruction that it involves.[2]

The source of the disaster is clear: it is a 'totally fraudulent notion of the physical universe', a vision obscured by 'the cataract of modern science'.

That sense of crisis puts art, his immediate subject, within a larger frame: the context of his writing becomes cosmological. Though his earlier writing – on Augustine, on the rupture in Western epistemology in the thirteenth century – always implied a cosmology that now becomes explicit. A perspective begins to open that leads him to the cosmologies of Pierre Teilhard de Chardin and Oskar Miłosz[3] and, ultimately, to the meaning of 'creation *ex nihilo*'.[4]

I

The discussion of art in *The Sacred in Life and Art* begins from positions already proposed in *The Rape of Man and Nature*. The first two chapters, 'Presuppositions of the Sacred' and 'The Sacrament', prepare the ground.

He has, though, to clarify once again his use of that word 'sacred'. For Sherrard, it is a word without meaning unless there is some concept of transcendence. He starts from a familiar definition: 'the sacred is something in which the Divine is present or which is

---

2. *Sacred in Life*, no page number.
3. The discussions of Teilhard de Chardin and Miłosz are chapters 5 and 6 in Sherrard's, *Human Image: World Image* (1992); 'The Meaning of Creation *ex nihilo*' is chapter 10 of his *Christianity: Lineaments of a Sacred Tradition* (1998).
4. The belief that God created the world *ex nihilo*, out of nothing, though not part of the formal creeds, has nevertheless been widely accepted in Christianity from the early centuries. It opposes the idea of creation '*ex materia*', out of some pre-existing substance distinct from God.

charged with divine energies',[5] but the sacred also requires a dimension of immanence. Unless the transcendent is somehow available in the immediacy of the world we could never perceive it; and only immanence can overcome epistemological dualism, the medieval split between the spiritual knowledge of revelation and empirical knowledge. Immanence plants God firmly in the world, but there is a danger of dualism in the terms themselves – transcendence *versus* immanence. That there are two terms – a duality – need not lead to a dualism unless they are in opposition. Sherrard approaches the problem by speaking of reciprocity, that perichoretic relation in which a duality does exist, but without becoming a dualism. Here the duality is that of God and creation:

> Nature – the psycho-physical realm – can be understood only when we recognize the reciprocal immanence of God and man, the uncreated and the created universe. But if there is no dichotomy, no dualism, there is duality. Dualism connotes the opposition, the externality of two units. It connotes irreducible pluralism with two terms. Duality on the other hand indicates the mutual completion of two units. It means two in one, two insofar as they go to make one.[6]

The radicalism of this view is the phrase 'the reciprocal immanence of God and man'. Immanence is generally understood as sourced in God, moving towards the human, towards the created world. Sherrard is suggesting that the human, the created, is as immanent within God as God is within the world. Only in that way can the duality be preserved, God as God and creation as creation; but only in that way can dualism be avoided and the unity of being be maintained.

---

5. *Sacred in Life*, p. 1.
6. *Sacred in Life*, p. 9.

That unity is essential for Sherrard; being, divine and human, created and uncreated, should be seen as one. For him, it is the failure of that unifying vision that infects the contemporary world, in the divorce of humanity from nature, of knowledge from vision, of the human from God. He adopts language from the 'alternative' culture of the mid-twentieth century: those who speak of humanity entering a new age, 'the age of Aquarius or the solar age', often, he says, use the word 'holistic', but the holistic is not just a way of looking at the world; for Sherrard it has its root in the being of God:

> Just as there can be nothing sacred without God, because ulti-
> mately God alone is sacred, so there can be no wholeness
> without God, because ultimately God alone is whole. It is
> God that is the principle and source of wholeness, and with-
> out participation in God there can be no escaping fragmenta-
> tion, disintegration, self-alienation, however much we may
> struggle against them.[7]

The alternative to wholeness, to the unifying vision, is fragmentation. The point, once again, is that the material world, including
the human, participates in the being of God, and can only be understood in that participation. This, Sherrard argues, is a 'sphere of
understanding' that 'lies far beyond that to which we are accus-
tomed, insofar as we think about these things at all'. There God is
an externality, an object apart:

> When people talk about God – and this is especially true in
> the Christian world – they often talk about Him as if he were
> a kind of object. And if they go on to talk about the relation-
> ship between God and the world, they often talk about it as
> being above all a relationship of cause and effect: God as a

---

7. *Sacred in Life*, p. 3.

world cause, a final cause or principle of being or existence; and the world and its laws are what he has produced.[8]

The offence, for Sherrard, is the externality: God there and humanity here. But the reality is an intimacy: 'God is never an object. He can be known only through Himself becoming the absolute subject of my own being.'[9]

At points in this discussion Sherrard shows himself aware of some of the tendencies in twentieth century theology. Again attacking externality, he rejects the idea of the divine as an 'irruption ... into the psychological and physical realm', the act of a God who is (echoing Karl Barth) 'the wholly Other'.[10] Without denying the otherness of God, Sherrard insists on the interpenetration of the divine and the human, of creation and the uncreated, of our sameness with that otherness. In speaking of the idea that humanity has now 'come of age' vis-à-vis God, he appears to echo Bonhoeffer.[11] But again he disagrees; implicit in that phrase is the idea of separation, of humanity moving into a realm apart from the being of God. For Sherrard there is no such separation.

II

These preliminary discussions establish some important features of Sherrard's theology. But what relevance do these ideas have for Sherrard's understanding of art?

---

8. *Sacred in Life*, p. 6.
9. *Sacred in Life*, p. 7.
10. *Sacred in Life*, p. 4. Karl Barth's insistence on God as 'wholly Other' is pervasive in his theology; but see (for example) his commentary on Question 25 of Calvin's Catechism, in Karl Barth, *The Faith of the Church* (London: Fontana Books, 1960), pp. 40–1.
11. Dietrich Bonhoeffer's belief that the situation of Christianity is changed in 'a world come of age' is developed (for example) in Dietrich Bonhoeffer, *Letters and Papers from Prison* (London: SCM Press, 1953), pp. 163–4.

Here there is a mediating concept, again drawn from his previous book: that of sacrament. It is for Sherrard the key to a full understanding of art. He uses the idea somewhat differently from its use in *The Rape of Man and Nature*. There the emphasis was on the universality of the sacramental: 'the created world is God's sacrament of Himself to Himself in His creatures.'[12] Sacrament is a universal category; all being is sacramental. In *The Sacred in Life and Art* the emphasis is on the particular instance of the sacramental; since all art is particular, is the thing that it is – poem or painting or music – sacrament must now be understood in relation to that particularity.

That is partly conveyed through his use of the word 'mystery'. Again, this recalls his earlier sympathy for the mystery religions of the ancient world. In the context of art, however, its power is to suggest a transformation particular to the act of creation. He uses the word 'mystery' to mean a point of entry into another mode of being. Although all existence has that potentiality, 'everything is capable of serving as the object of the sacrament, for everything is intrinsically consecrated and divine – is, in fact, intrinsically a *mysterium*'[13] – there has to be a moment of revelation and of recognition. That is the moment of art. Art reveals what is universally true in the particularity of this object, these words, these images.

Sherrard recognises that art does not work in generalities but in particularities, such as Seferis's statues, the old men of Yeats's jade sculpture. Every revelation of the sacramental nature of being, whether liturgical or artistic is unique. The sacramental, the interpenetration of created and uncreated, cannot be relegated to a theological principle or to an inert general category:

This essential likeness or congeneracy between uncreated and created does not mean, however, that the object and

---

12. *Rape of Man*, p. 94.
13. *Sacred in Life*, p. 23.

action of the sacrament are a matter of indifference or that they can be indiscriminately exchanged. Every sacrament is absolutely unique in its significance; it is something which in spite or, rather, because of its universal nature is singled out and set apart, unexchangeable and unrepeatable.[14]

The work of art, if it is truly a work of art, is also 'unexchangeable', an 'unrepeatable' moment of recognition.

The discussion up to this point sets the terms for Sherrard's exploration of the nature of art. There is the interpenetration of the divine and the material, the *perichoresis* of uncreated and created that he has explored in his previous book. There is its expression in sacrament, at those points where divine and material reveal themselves, not in dualism, but in mutually participating duality. That unity must be made visible. For Sherrard, that is the goal of all art; and the artist is, for him, a hieratic figure, sacramentally revealing the universal in the particular.

III

To make that plain Sherrard must take issue with contemporary understandings of art, and he does so through an engagement with an antagonist, the philosopher of modernism Herbert Read.[15] In the third chapter of *The Sacred in Life and Art*, 'The Artist and the Sacred: Where the Battle Lies', he sets out the nature of their conflict. His starting point is an essay that Read wrote for the monthly magazine *Encounter*.[16] At first there is agreement: Read had deplored both the current state of the arts and their prospects. 'The arts', he said, 'fight a losing battle in our technological civilization', and Sherrard agrees, but they disagree on their response. For Read, the only resource is

14. *Sacred in Life*, p. 24.
15. Herbert Read (1893–1968) was a poet and a historian and philosopher of art. He was also a leading English Jungian.
16. Herbert Read, 'Testament' (*Encounter*, 19 (4), October 1962).

attack, to continue the fight for art, otherwise 'we retreat into despair, silence or some Dirt-dump'. What the artist must not do is walk away: 'every writer who retires to an Aegean Island' is committing 'desertion of the front line of our fragmented and alienated societies'.[17]

Sherrard holds his hand up: 'harsh words, especially to the ears of one who has "retired" to an Aegean island'.[18] But Read has mis-diagnosed the problem. To expect art of any human depth from a culture that has lost its spiritual roots is vain. No amount of front-line resistance will produce what is not there. For Sherrard, art of substance presupposes the metaphysical; a culture that has cut its links with its metaphysical roots will produce a limited and impoverished art. A culture that sees human beings only 'as realities that exist in their own right' has severed such roots:

> Western art of the last few centuries is for the most part a reflection of this way of looking at things. It is a record of what happens when man tries to live as though he were a self-subsistent being of psyche and sense and as though the universe is not multi-structured but to all intents and purposes limited to the purely psychological and physical dimensions.[19]

The only answer, for Sherrard, is the recovery of metaphysical roots, which, in the case of the Western world means Christianity, but tacitly accepts that such a renewal is unlikely. The language of that tradition is, for the most part, unavailable or dead. What then can the artist do?

Sherrard admits that the task is very difficult. The contemporary artist lives in a culture that has largely excluded the metaphysical. The resources of an earlier time, the language and the symbols that embodied a metaphysical view, cannot simply be summoned back

---

17. *Sacred in Life*, p. 32.
18. Ibid. Sherrard had bought a property at Katounia near Limni on the Greek island of Evia in 1959 and subsequently made it his home.
19. *Sacred in Life*, p. 33.

into existence. Just to adopt the language of tradition, to create a self-consciously 'Christian' poetry against the grain of the time, will not work. To adopt the spirituality itself might appear to be a solution (he is thinking of Eliot's conversion to Anglicanism), 'but one wonders whether it is so simple':

> An artist must by definition make use of a language, pictorial, musical or verbal. If his art is to function, this language must be alive, dynamic, rooted in the artist's own experience and sensitivity. Moreover, it must be a language that communicates, if not to the whole of a given society, at least to those sections of it with which the artist in some way identifies himself.[20]

For the present-day artist these conditions are unlikely to be fulfilled; and an artist 'cannot function in a vacuum'.

So where is the artist to turn, to reach beyond the assumptions of an essentially non-metaphysical society? Sherrard is clear that this cannot be resolved on the level of the artist's material, and is not a matter of discovering a new (or old) idiom. What is required is some mode of spiritual discipline, a reaching within for resources that contemporary society disregards. This may even involve a renunciation of art as we know it:

> It may indeed be that the only positive course now available for the artist is one of retreat from the cultural battle, retreat not into despair or some dirt-dump but into silence or into what Yeats has called 'our proper dark', that chaos or abyss of pre-formal possibilities in which he may come to know the pre-artistic (because unmanifest) sources of spiritual energy from which our world is increasingly estranged.[21]

---

20. *Sacred in Life*, p. 37.
21. *Sacred in Life*, p. 35.

The language is Jungian, but also suggests Sherrard's writing on the monastic life on Mount Athos. He insists, elsewhere in this chapter, on contemplation,[22] but the inward journey is dangerous, not a settling into some consoling unity; it is, for Sherrard, 'dark'. Yet, it is there that all art is rooted, in a profound self-knowledge, in an opening of the self to what it really is:

> To discern where and in what forms the voice of eternity speaks in the broken accents of a disinherited time and place … demands an unflinching truth to one's own inner being and to the language that comes as genuinely, as non-artificially, from one's soul as the tree from the earth.[23]

Such an inward descent, always possible whatever the cultural environment, may even produce 'moments of revelation and illumination, intimations and intuitions of eternity, and so transfigure the material of art with that beauty and rhythm which are the hallmark of the sacred'.[24]

The last sentence carries echoes of Wordsworth; and it might be objected that art, at least since the Romantic period, has been built around such inner journeys, such explorations of the self. Is Sherrard demanding a return to a Romantic aesthetic? Though he points the artist back to inwardness, he is not advocating an art of self-expression. That, for him, is one of the failures of art in the modern world: it produces endless individualism, an inwardness of ungrounded subjectivity in which the novelty of each new 'voice' is sufficient justification.

Sherrard's argument with Read continues in the fourth chapter, 'Modern Art and the Heresy of Humanism'. At first it seems as though Sherrard and Read are very close. Sherrard traces Read's

---

22. *Sacred in Life*, p. 51.
23. *Sacred in Life*, p. 38.
24. *Sacred in Life*, p. 40.

development as a philosopher of art to his early identification of 'instinct' or 'intuition' as the artist's source. It is there that the 'first inkling of truth' arises. Against the over-cerebral, over-controlled art of a poet such as Eliot, the mind of the artist needs to look elsewhere, beneath what the conscious mind has to offer. For Read, 'the mind, given the raw material, works unconsciously to create':[25]

> This led [Read] directly to Freud and Jung, for in their concept of the unconscious he saw a possible source for the raw material of art as well as its shaping agent. From now on psychology – and in his later years almost exclusively Jungian psychology – was to provide a basis indispensable to his aesthetics.[26]

So where, then, is the point of difference? Read appears to offer the inward journey that Sherrard requires, the confrontation with the darkness of the self that is the source of art. Sherrard and Read (and Jung) even share the same language of archetypes.

For Sherrard, the difference has to do with metaphysics. Without a metaphysical structure the deliverances of the inward self, its drives and dynamics, remain what they are, unstructured and unshaped. He suggests that Read may himself have been uncertain that such drives can generate the coherence of art. 'It became increasingly difficult for him to accept that archetypes possess any formal coherence or any coherence that can be expressed only in a specific form or in a form already known. Thus for him archetypes are essentially formless predispositions and nothing more.'[27] Art that is no more than the mouthpiece of the archetypes may produce something vivid, even something that connects with the same archetypes in its audience; but without a

---

25. *Sacred in Life*, p. 42.
26. *Sacred in Life*, p. 43.
27. *Sacred in Life*, p. 49.

metaphysics it will lack the form that, for art, is also truth. The predictable outcome of Read's theory might be Surrealism, the art form that was dominant during his formative years; Sherrard makes that connection in his 1983 discussion of Elytis.[28] For Sherrard, the inner self, the self the artist comes to know in contemplation, stands in mutuality with an embracing metaphysical truth; and it is from that mutuality that its sacramental life derives.

Sherrard is clear that for art some metaphysical frame is required; without it there can be 'no ultimate reality, no complete truth, nothing of a trans-historical nature that had been given to man through revelation and could be known equally well at all times and in every place'.[29] Sherrard seems to be referring the artist to some formalised doctrine, to some *credo*. Though doctrine may be involved, Sherrard is not looking to a set of propositions. Whatever may be known of that 'trans-historical' truth, to be art it must always flow from and return to life. To speak of metaphysics,

> does not mean of course that I have to subject my imagination to a set of abstract concepts and rational propositions. Doctrine – religious doctrine – is not abstract or rational. It is symbolic and metaphorical. And what it symbolizes or is a metaphor for are not abstract ideas or principles or laws but living beings.[30]

Here Sherrard suggests, as he had done as early as his 1951 lecture on St Symeon, that all relationship with truth is a relationship of persons. Something like a paradox emerges, one with which he would have been entirely happy: all art is personal, but it should not be an expression of individualism. Individualism in art invests in difference; the personal draws on a common metaphysical ground that moves toward a unity of vision.

---

28. See footnote 45 below.
29. *Sacred in Life*, p. 46.
30. *Sacred in Life*, p. 48.

IV

Against that background, what is Sherrard to make of the creations of art, of the panoply of artefacts that define all cultures? What is he to make of diversity and change in art? If true art is always oriented to an unchanging metaphysical reality, why should change ever appear?

Here Sherrard finds himself addressing the matter of evolution. Contemporary views of art, such as that of Herbert Read, assume that art evolves just as thought or technology evolve; that some progressive process is at work, a forward movement from what was to what will be. Sherrard regularly attacks this view, and not just in the context of art; he does so most directly in the third chapter of *Human Image: World Image*.[31] At points he seems to reject the idea of evolution as generally understood. His target, though, is not biology, but the dominance in all areas of the evolutionary model, of the assumption that the processes of evolution must always apply. He associates this with a particular image of time, time as a 'linear axis' moving from past to future, one we call 'history'. The evolutionary model assumes that movement along that axis is not just change but progression, an advance from the less to the more. On that basis, the thinking of the present devalues the thinking of the past. Because it stands at an earlier point on the axis of progression, it must be of lesser value.

Sherrard sees this attachment to evolutionary progression as a corollary of the absence of any secure metaphysical base. Without that, meaning must be found along the axis of linear time; there must be a progression towards some fuller truth, a progression of which change itself is the motor. Newness and difference then become values in their own right. Out of that comes the elevation, in the world of art, of the avant-garde:

31. 'The Apotheosis of Time and the Bogey of Evolution', in Philip Sherrard, *Human Image: World Image* (1992), pp. 56–76.

One has, in Rimbaud's words, to be absolutely modern. This among other things means that one has to be a member of the avant-garde, that very special group of people probing forward into the unknown and gleaning from the formless depths of their unconscious fragmentary images of the future. Read himself was convinced that a number of special artists in his time – including Klee, Kandinsky, Mondrian, Gabo, Moore and Picasso – had thus shaped the foundation of a cultural regeneration.[32]

It is implicit in this view that human consciousness is itself evolving. That has the effect of relativising not only the thought of the past, but also the thought of the present; both are imperfect versions of some fully evolved consciousness that human beings will, at some point, attain.

Sherrard sees art as faced with a choice. It can either understand itself as part of the axis of evolution or it can seek a grounding in some stable truth. Here, once again, he turns to Plato, conventionally not known as a champion of the arts. In chapter five, 'Art and Originality', Sherrard recalls Plato's objections to the artist, the one who mistakes appearance for reality, who is so involved in the immediacy of the world that eternal truth is ignored. But that, Sherrard argues, is not the whole of Plato; there is space for an acceptable art. If false art distracts its audience from the real and consigns people to illusion, there is an art that 'celebrates the praises of the gods', that directs itself 'not to the appearances of reality or to [the artist's] reactions to them, but to reality itself'.[33]

Here Sherrard finds a position close to his own. Just as Plato's eternal forms are unchanging, so for Sherrard there is an eternal metaphysical truth that is also unchanging and that it is the

---

32. *Sacred in Life*, p. 52.
33. *Sacred in Life*, p. 58.

purpose of art to reveal. There can therefore be no progression in art, only greater or lesser success in attaining its object. Ideas of progress and evolution in art must be an 'absurdity' to anyone capable of artistic response,

> for there is not and cannot be any criterion according to which it is possible to demonstrate that the artefacts of our modern civilization evince a higher degree of intelligence, beauty or of any other positive quality than, say, an Egyptian temple, the poetry of Homer and the Book of Kells.[34]

For Sherrard, all art stands equidistant from truth, from its metaphysical grounding; which is something that the evolutionary model implicitly denies.

The decisive instance of this equidistance is, for Sherrard, the icon. In chapter six, 'The Art of the Icon', Sherrard presents the icon as normative for the comprehension of art. Again, the central argument has to do with time.

Whereas Read and modernists understand works of art largely through their position on the linear, progressive axis, Sherrard argues that the icon steps out of that linearity to realise a time of its own. Because the icon can be approached only within the context from which it emerges, which is the context of liturgy, it shares the time of liturgy. Liturgy does not inhabit past or present; or perhaps it inhabits both. It repeats, speaks words that have already been spoken in the same form and pattern, invokes presences that do not change. Consequently,

> Since these celebrations and the events composing them are homologous with each other, and these events are personalized, it follows that all this together must mean that the time

---

34. *Sacred in Life*, p. 50.

to which liturgy introduces us is not that in which one moment succeeds another, each disappearing into a vanishing and irreversible past.[35]

Liturgy – and hence the icon – stands outside linear time. Consequently it cannot be a 'memorial' of the past, because that would be to situate it in that time, a present against a past. Pastness is here irrelevant: 'the events – which are persons – that the liturgy evokes do not occur in the past: they occur in the present which is their time.'[36] The works of art that Sherrard sees as incomparably great – Dante's *Divina Commedia*, Chartres Cathedral, the Taj Mahal, the wall-paintings of Ajanta, the Byzantine Church of St Saviour in Hora, the music of India, the Tudor masters[37] – share that with the icon: they create a time of their own.

The icon can be what it is only because, unlike much contemporary art, it has a metaphysical grounding. At the heart of Sherrard's understanding of the icon is its source. The icon begins in a vision of spiritual truth, and that vision controls what the icon is. It is not determined by the personality or subjectivity of the artist or the demands of pictorial representation. It stands apart from the contemporary perception of art as self-expression, as the individual 'voice':

> The icon is based on a very different understanding of things. It is based on the idea that a spiritual vision expresses itself necessarily in a certain formal language. ... Far from the individual artist choosing the form, it is the spiritual reality that is to be expressed which itself chooses, or imposes, the form in which the artist must express it.[38]

---

35. *Sacred in Life*, p. 83.
36. *Sacred in Life*, p. 83–4.
37. This list appears in the final chapter of *Sacred in Life*, p. 142.
38. *Sacred in Life*, p. 80.

The making of an icon must, therefore, depend on a spiritual discipline that can lead to that vision: 'the artist has to become one with that which he is to represent'. And that becoming one is rooted in contemplation: 'there is here no distinction between art and contemplation. ... There has to be an endless recreation within the life of the artist of the spiritual realities which are the subject of his work.'[39]

So understood, the icon stands apart from other forms of art. 'If the icon is a work of art, it is not one which is similar in kind to other works of art.'[40] Yet, it may remain a point of reference for all art in the most important respects. It can be properly encountered only within the context from which it arises and to which it returns. It creates a time of its own. It does not 'express' the artist. Most vitally, it begins from vision, a vision that grows from the contemplation of those spiritual realities in which the artist, like all human beings, is a participant.

V

Yet, there is still the question of diversity in art; Sherrard has his preferences, poets for whom he feels most affinity. This raises again the matter of Romanticism and his affinity with it; this is because the English-language poets to whom he returns, whom he most often names, are Blake and Yeats, who are both loosely identified as Romantics.[41]

These represent a particular mode of Romanticism, distinct in important ways from Wordsworth, Keats or Shelley. Blake and Yeats have an overriding aim: they use their poetry to realise a vision. They each pursue a metaphysical truth that determines their art. In

---

39. *Sacred in Life*, p. 82.
40. *Sacred in Life*, p. 71.
41. In his correspondence with George Seferis, in *This Dialogue of Blood and Light*, George Seferis and Philip Sherrard mention Blake 16 times and Yeats 13 times. They mention Shelley four times, Wordsworth and Keats three times, and Byron twice.

that, they are attempting what Sherrard sees as the goal of all art. If Sherrard is a Romantic, it is in that company that he belongs.[42]

Art as vision is the focus of the final chapter, 'Vision of the Sacred', of Sberrard's *The Sacred in Life and Art*. Here he summarises his understanding of art; and he returns to a word not used before in this book but central to much of his earlier writing, the word 'gnosis'. That he now places in intimate relation to the word 'sacred': 'the quality that distinguishes a work of sacred art is I think one that can be described only by a word like knowledge, or gnosis.'[43] Sacred art is knowledge, and what it knows is truth:

> Sacred art is a mode of knowing the Truth. It is a mode of knowing the Truth because it is the revelation of the Truth, its prophecy or its epiphany. Hence sacred art is not so much the expression of a human intimation or of an aspiration for the Divine as the Divine itself revealing itself through the human. It is a gift of God of which the artist is the vehicle.[44]

This 'gnosis' is a mode of vision: a completeness of vision in which the entire human capacity for knowing is involved.

It is now clear what Sherrard means by the sacred. It is what is revealed in 'gnosis', in that holistic vision. For him the artist is the great revealer; it is the artist who makes the mutuality of the divine and the material visible. In that revelation the personality of the artist is lost, with no reality apart from its participation in the reality that it reveals.

That view finds its fullest expression in an uncollected essay that Sherrard published in 1983, a discussion of the poetry of Odysseus

---

42. To the names of Blake and Yeats might be added that of Swedenborg, another visionary, who receives some attention in Sherrard's next book, *Human Image: World Image* (1992).
43. *Sacred in Life*, p. 130.
44. *Sacred in Life*, p. 130.

Elytis.[45] Sherrard makes extensive use of Elytis's own writing on art and poetry; and what emerges is a strong affinity. Elytis, like Sherrard, understands art as vision and the artist as visionary; again, like Sherrard, he sees art as the means to reach beyond the rationalism of the Western world.

That is where the discussion begins. Elytis's early poetry, of the 1930s, was written under the influence of surrealism, particularly French surrealist poetry; and both Elytis and Sherrard see surrealism as a direct counter to rationalism. Sherrard quotes Elytis: he saw it as his task 'to destroy the tradition of rationalism which lay heavily on the Western world'. Sherrard has his own understanding of surrealism: the withdrawal of the rational and the logical allows a vision to emerge that is less the expression of Jungian drives and archetypes, more that of the visionary spirit. Surrealism becomes, for him, an agent of 'gnosis'. He finds support for that in Elytis, who says that the poet 'makes the invisible visible, spiritual realities perceptible, the non-concrete concrete'. In language that is strikingly close to Sherrard's, he marks out those poets who 'express directly their impulsion towards the vision of Paradise' and whose work 'is the endless course toward the natural light that is the Divine Logos, and the uncreated light that is God'.

Sherrard finds much else to praise in Elytis. He admires Elytis's power, like that of Seferis, to construct a mythology out of the elements of the world. He points to the poem 'Aegean' (1940):

Already a whole mythology is being delineated, its archetypal figures are being born: Eros, sea, islands, ships, the wind, the woman on the rock, the feminine being who is the all-

---

45. Philip Sherrard, 'Odysseus Elytis and the Discovery of Greece', *Journal for Modern Greek Studies*, 1 (2), October 1983, pp. 271–93. Referred to subsequently as 'Odysseus Elytis'. Sherrard brought out his joint translations of Elytis in Edmund Keeley and Philip Sherrard, *Odysseus Elytis: Selected* Poems (Harmondsworth: Penguin, 1981).

pervasive, all-embracing haunter of this world. ... It is as though a liturgy were being celebrated in which are invoked not the names of saints or the events of a metaphysical world, but the most humble things that surround us.[46]

Elytis creates a world of imagination; he is not, Sherrard insists, a nature poet. It is an imagination that encompasses the materiality of the world, but it begins from an inner reality of which the outer world is an analogue. The eye sees through the imagination, and what it sees is 'the images that pre-exist'. The vision of a poet like Elytis is an *anamnesis*, a recovery from forgetfulness of the already known, a realisation in verbal form of the true nature of both the external world and the inner. In a passage that contains as much of himself as it does of Elytis, Sherrard says:

> The Greece of the imagination is not simply a representation or description in poetic language of the natural beauty of Greece, nor are the images of his poetry merely metaphors through which his experiences of the natural Greek world may be communicated to others. Rather it is the other way about: the world of the imagination – the world of incorporeal images – is a world in its own right, and it is of this world that things in the natural world – the things we can see and touch – are the metaphors or, to use the language of Paracelsus and Boehme, the signatures.

Elytis speaks of 'the just correlation of the physical and the spiritual world', which raises the sensible world to 'a level that is sacred'.[47]

In *The Sacred in Life and Art*, Sherrard explored the sacred in relation to art and the artist. It is for him, as it was for Elytis, a matter

---

46. 'Odysseus Elytis', p. 281–2.
47. 'Odysseus Elytis', p. 283.

of vision; in the conclusion of the essay he speaks, not surprisingly, of Blake and the need to 'cleanse the doors of perception'. It is only through such vision that dualisms can be overcome. He goes back to some words of Seferis, that Greece is confined by the rocks of the Symplegades through which the Argonauts had to make their perilous way. But he applies that image to Elytis, to the search for a unifying vision: 'the rocks stand for all those contradictions and oppositions by which our lives in this world are usually so crushed and shut in, and which prevent us from ever reaching our true self: here and there, right and wrong, past and future.'[48] In Sherrard's next book, *Human Image: World Image*, the full requirements of such a view are laid out. Any vision that aspires to completeness must, in the end, confront the question of being itself; must, in short, become cosmological.

---

48. 'Odysseus Elytis', p. 286.

7

A Cosmology of Persons

Human Image: World Image, published in 1992, is Philip Sherrard's most difficult book.[1] The difficulty derives from its subject: the relation between cosmology and anthropology, between our understanding of the universe as a whole and our understanding of ourselves. At its heart is the pursuit of a sacred cosmology, one that unifies the material world and the spiritual, that reveals the co-inherence of the created and the uncreated. Within that, a central theme emerges: the place of persons in the totality of being. Sherrard develops a cosmology in which persons, the loving, valuing beings we find ourselves to be, are more than a function of an essentially mechanical process but the key to the process. It is in knowing ourselves as persons that we come to know all else, can approach a cosmological vision. Sherrard's earlier concerns – the sacred, the problem of dualism – are held within that wider frame. What would the fullest account of all-that-is be like? And what would our place, as humanity, be within it?

He develops his discussion in stages. First, there is a review of pre-Renaissance cosmologies. Then follow three chapters in which he examines the foundations of the normative contemporary cosmology –

---

1. Philip Sherrard, *Human Image: World Image* (Ipswich: Golgonooza Press, 1992). Reissued Denise Harvey (Publisher), Limni, Evia, Greece, 2004. Referred to subsequently as *Human Image*.

mathematics, time and the evolutionary model. After that he explores the cosmologies of two twentieth-century thinkers, Pierre Teilhard de Chardin and Oskar Miłosz. Finally, in 'Notes Towards the Restitution of Sacred Cosmology', he sketches a cosmology of his own.

The kind of cosmology that he is exploring in this book is not the physical cosmology offered by science, the 'Big Bang', the expansion of space and time. Our place in that cosmology is that we are a function of the process. Sherrard's cosmology insists on human participation, on the cosmologically integral nature of the human person. Such a cosmology can be formed only as myth, to be understood as transcendental truth in narrative form. Myth is not failed science, but it is the expression of a truth of relation in which the human person has a place. It is as myth, not as science, that Sherrard scrutinises the cosmologies of Teilhard de Chardin and Miłosz.

I

Sherrard opens the book by stressing the importance of these apparently remote issues for the most pressing of human problems: the ecological crisis. Though not the first time he has pointed to these dangers, he has never done so with such force as in this Introduction. There is anger and frustration, a near-despair at the failure of the world to take the risks seriously. Sherrard strikes this note in his first paragraph:

> One thing at least we no longer need to be told is that we are in the throes of a crisis of the most appalling dimensions. We tend to call this crisis the ecological crisis. ... Our entire way of life is humanly and environmentally suicidal, and unless we change it radically there is no way in which we can avoid cosmic catastrophe. Without such change the whole adventure of civilization will come to an end during the lifetime of many now living.[2]

---

2. *Human Image*, p. 1.

To that threat there has been no adequate response. Conservation in its various forms is important, but more basic changes are needed: 'unless that happens, conservation theory and practice, however well-intentioned and necessary, will not touch the heart of the problem.'[3]

How then does that become a cosmological issue, not just an issue concerning the management of the earth? And why link cosmology with anthropology, as Sherrard does? He offers an initial answer, which explains the title of the book:

> How we see the world depends above all upon how we see ourselves. Our model of the universe – our world-picture or world image – is based upon the model we have of ourselves, upon our own self-image. When we look at the world, what we see is a reflection of our own mind, our own mode of consciousness. Our perception of a tree, a mountain, a face, an animal or a bird is a reflection of our idea of who we think we are.[4]

Nor is our idea of ourselves a given; human beings have choices, have lived from very different self-images. But within modern culture that has been forgotten in the dominance of a particular paradigm: one that 'impels us to look upon ourselves as little more than two-legged animals ... whose destiny and needs can best be fulfilled through the pursuit of social, political and economic self-interest'. Within that paradigm and following from it, 'nature is seen as an impersonal commodity, a soulless source of food, raw materials, wealth, power.'[5]

The source of the crisis is a self-perception that makes our destructive practices appear logical and even necessary, but that anthropology generates a cosmology. There has, Sherrard argues, been a

---

3. *Human Image*, p. 2.
4. Ibid.
5. *Human Image*, p. 3.

communal act of forgetfulness: modern humanity has forgotten what most humanity, historically, believed it knew about its place in the universe. 'In the great creative cultures of the world, human beings do not regard themselves as two-legged animals. ... On the contrary, they think of themselves first and foremost as descended from the gods, or from God, and as heirs to eternity, with a destiny that goes far beyond politics, society and economics.'[6]

That view led to a very different relationship to nature. We tend to think, Sherrard suggests, that the reason traditional societies did not use the world as we do, dominating it and exploiting its resources, was because they lacked the power to do so; the implication being that, had they had the power, they would have behaved as we do. Yes, they made use of nature:

> They may trade in the gifts [nature offers] – in precious stones and spices, in corn and cattle. They may in ignorance be excessive in their demands on them, in grazing their flocks or in felling too many trees. But they did not deliberately *trade in nature itself*, or at the expense of nature.[7]

Nature was not a commodity; they perceived the natural order as in some sense God-given and therefore sacred, an idea 'characterized nowadays as primitive, as based on superstition', held by only those 'who have failed, for whatever reason, to move into the twentieth century'.[8] Sherrard detects what he had identified in *The Sacred in Life and Art*: this is the power of an evolutionary model by which the ideas of the past are dismissed simply because they are of the past.

Such a parochialism of the present is inclined to dismiss what Sherrard calls 'the other mind of Europe', the tradition of philos-

---

6. *Human Image*, p. 4.
7. *Human Image*, p. 5.
8. *Human Image*, pp. 5–6.

ophers 'from Plato to Berdyaev' and poets 'from Homer to Yeats'.[9] The past should have its voice. But his deeper demand is for a cosmology that will restore the human relationship with the universe. One obstacle is that science claims to offer a reality that is objective and value-free, one that carries no metaphysical presuppositions. Values exist, but they belong elsewhere, to the private realm of our own subjectivity; and scientists, 'insofar as they are scientists claim to operate independently of value-judgements'. That, however, is humanly impossible. 'The very nature of human thought is such that it cannot operate independently of value-judgements, assumptions and dogmas. Even the assertion that it can constitutes a value-judgement and implies a whole philosophy, whether we are aware of it or not.'[10]

Science may concede that values have some reality; there may be something beyond its value-free methodology. It is not 'intended to deny that there is, or may be, another aspect of things – that which is spiritual and eternal and unextended in time and space – that can also be studied in its own right and could be said to constitute the sphere of spiritual knowledge or of a spiritual science'.[11] That concession, rarely observed in practice, immediately opens a dualism. 'There are not two sciences, the one concerned with the material and outward aspect of things extended in time and space, and the other with their spiritual and eternal dimension, unextended in time and space. There is only one science.'[12] That 'one science' is what Sherrard means by a cosmology, but from where might such a cosmology come? Again, he makes the link with anthropology. A true understanding of the whole is dependent on a true understanding of ourselves, of what we are, of the sacredness of our being:

---

9. *Human Image*, p. 132.
10. *Human Image*, p. 7.
11. *Human Image*, p. 7.
12. *Human Image*, p. 8.

A false self-view breeds a false world-view, and together they breed our nemesis and the nemesis of the world. Once we repossess a sense of our own holiness, we will recover the sense of the holiness of the world about us as well, and we will then act towards the world about us with the awe and humility that we should possess when we enter a sacred shrine.[13]

II

Driven by that urgency, Sherrard begins his cosmological explorations. The first chapter of the book, 'Forms of Sacred Cosmology in the Pre-Renaissance World', is a historical survey, but it is also a counter to that parochialism of the present that he had identified in the 'Introduction'. The ideas of the past are worth present consideration; without them we may fail to understand our own situation. On that basis Sherrard sets out to explore these ancient perspectives.

In this discussion he applies two tests. The first is dualism: does this cosmology create a dualistic view of reality? The other has to do with persons: does this view give adequate weight to personhood, to the human subject in relation to the totality of being? Both tests are stringently applied; both result in some adjustment of Sherrard's previous positions.

This is clearest in the first part of the chapter, in his discussion of Plato's cosmology. Plato had always been important to Sherrard, from the letters and essays of the 1940s[14] to *The Greek East and the Latin West* in 1959. There he saw in Plato a unitary vision of being, a golden chain of existence connecting the forms to the entities of the world available to the senses. Through the interpenetration of forms and material entities, all being was one. Now in 1992 his reading of Plato is more complex. He addresses a suspicion, one that

---

13. *Human Image*, p. 9.
14. Plato is referred to 27 times in Sherrard's early essays and correspondence with George Seferis.

he has held since at least 1959, that Plato too may be guilty of dualism. He makes a distinction between the earlier Plato and the later. He sees the earlier Plato as influenced by the Pythagoreans. Sherrard says of him that he 'inherited from the Pythagoreans the idea that the reality of things in the physical or natural world ... is geometrical in structure or form'. [15] The forms are to be conceived of mathematically, and so have a mathematical intelligibility. If that is the case, then only the forms are truly intelligible; and if reality is identified with intelligibility, a radical dualism begins to open:

> In one aspect of Plato's thought emphasis on the transcendence of the intelligible world of pure forms is pushed so far that to all intents and purposes the physical world appears to be stripped of all reality whatsoever. Only the intelligible is real, and the intelligible is not physical at all. [16]

Such an emphasis would result in 'a complete gulf between the world accessible to the senses – the world of nature – and ... the transcendent world of pure forms, in which alone reality is to be found'. [17]

In *The Greek East and the Latin West*, sensing this problem, Sherrard had suggested that the overarching reality, the Good, which was beyond both forms and the material world, resolved the apparent dualism. [18] Now he suggests that the later Plato, from the *Phaedrus* on and especially in the *Timaeus*, attempted to overcome dualism by introducing the idea of Soul, 'the origin of movement', which 'moves after the pattern of the immutable intelligible world' and is therefore the principle of order in the cosmos. [19] Since the coming-to-be of the

---

15. *Human Image*, p. 12.
16. Ibid.
17. Ibid.
18. *Greek East and Latin West*, p. 6.
19. *Human Image*, p. 13.

material world requires movement, this Soul as the origin of movement must be present in the being of all that is as the 'Soul of the World', and that must include human existence. Sherrard argues that in this later Platonic perspective all being is 'ensouled'; there is no radical division between the eternal and the temporal.

So, it is suggested, Plato escapes from his dualistic tendencies: form and materiality are no longer in opposition. But if Plato has been saved from dualism, Sherrard's other test also applies: is this a cosmology that gives proper place to personhood and humanity as subject? Here he finds Plato less defensible. The 'World Soul' that connects the forms with the materiality of existence seems to equate to the Demiurge, the Platonic God who brings about the existence of the world. This God is impersonal. It has no place for the person and remains 'something external to and independent of him', an impersonal source of cosmic order that must be recognised and obeyed. In this Platonic cosmology,

> What is important for God is not the single person but the whole. ... What is important is the cosmic order. This the single person could in no way disturb. His part is to learn the divine plan, to obey it, to adjust himself to it, to become one with the cosmic order. But whether he does or not is a matter of indifference to the order itself.[20]

Sherrard is clearly looking towards Christianity, with its placing of persons at the centre, but he is making a more general point. A cosmology that leaves personhood aside, that sees the human subject as one object in an impersonal universe, is an inadequate vision of being as a whole.

Sherrard finds the cosmology of Stoicism faulty by the same test. Yes, it affirms a monism, overcomes dualism by seeing the cosmos

---

20. *Human Image*, p. 16.

as 'a great living organism', single and self-sustained; yes, it allows for a divine element, the 'seed-sowing Logos' that permeates all being in different degrees. Yet all is essentially impersonal, and

> man is forced to regard himself as inevitably and inextricably in bondage to the impersonal, materialized and embodied forms of existence in which he is involved ... All he could achieve was a state of noble indifference or unruffled impassivity in the face of all that happens, for good or ill, for joy or sorrow, in the prison-house in which he is subjected to forces entirely beyond his control.[21]

The only human choice (which affects nothing) is to endure.

There was, however, a tradition in the ancient world that Sherrard sees as giving primacy to the person, and that was the Mystery tradition. He is thinking of Eleusis and similar cults, Dionysian and Orphic. Here the aim was a direct and personal relationship to the god and a resulting transformation of the self:

> In an intimate relationship, in a vital union with his god, the initiate participates in another life. The rites of the various Mysteries give the pattern of the mystic drama, a divine progress which is the principle and prototype of salvation. ... They gave, by sudden illumination, foretaste of a numinous reality.[22]

Sherrard makes an immediate connection to Christianity: the Mysteries 'have been called imitative anticipations of the Christian mystery'. Like the Eucharist, they placed the individual at the centre of a drama of death and rebirth. He finds an echo in Christ's words:

---

21. *Human Image*, pp. 16–17.
22. *Human Image*, p. 23.

'Verily, verily, I say unto you, except a corn of wheat fall into the earth and die, it abides alone; but if it die, it brings forth much fruit'.[23]

Sherrard, however, rejects the cosmology of the Mysteries. Their aim is absorption into the god; all being is to be fused with the being of the god, who is all. Dualism is overcome; but this for him is another false monism. If the Platonic 'World Soul' and the Stoics consigned the human person to cosmic irrelevance, the Mysteries dissolved the person into a higher being as it vanishes into the god. That, for Sherrard, is false to our experience; we know our own reality. 'Spiritual identity' is not attained 'by ceasing to be human'.[24] In the Christian view, the relation between God and each person is one of reciprocity, in which the reality of each is preserved: 'God is born in man and man is born in God. The humanity remains within the divinity, the divinity within the humanity. We are not asked to abandon our created human nature. ... Nothing of the living person, of the unique creature, is to be sacrificed.'[25] When the Orthodox Church speaks of 'deification' as the goal of human life, it does not mean the transformation of the human into God with no remainder. It means the full realisation of the reciprocity that already exists, the mutuality of participation that is the true relation of the human to the divine and the essence of personhood.

Sherrard returns, then, to participation – to *perichoresis* – as the foundation of a true cosmology. The human subject has its existence within such a mutuality, within its reciprocity with the divine. To speak of 'individuals' is a matter of counting, essentially mathematical; to be a person is to find oneself within a relationship where there is duality but no dualism, where the being of each is sustained and completed by the being of the other. This for Sherrard is central to any understanding of the human within the cosmos.

---

23. John 12:24.
24. *Human Image*, p. 26.
25. *Human Image*, p. 26.

III

The next three chapters of *Human Image: World Image* are one argument: they are Sherrard's critique of the basic assumptions of the contemporary world view, the assumed cosmology of the Western world. Again, the tests are dualism and the place of the person; and, as with the ancient cosmologies, Sherrard finds the modern view inadequate. He addresses himself to three principal constituents of this cosmology – the place of mathematics, evolution as a model of change, and the understanding of time. In all of that he is looking, once again, to extend the knowable beyond the bounds set by the current world view.

He begins with the primacy given to mathematics as both the instrument and the substance of the knowable. Sherrard's broad case is clear. Mathematics has become the only certain knowledge, and whatever claims to be knowledge must be expressible in mathematical terms. Such a model moves necessarily towards abstraction, and consequently all that is not abstraction – the texture of lived experience – falls out of consideration.

Sherrard begins from the scientific revolution of the sixteenth and seventeenth centuries. At that point medieval cosmology, which saw the world as 'a sacred order established by God' in which all things were 'expressions of a divine harmony, symbols linking the visible and the invisible, earth and heaven'[26], was displaced. The agents of this change, 'men like Kepler, Galileo, Descartes and Newton', were all mathematicians, and so the cosmology that grew around them was a mathematical cosmology. God became 'the great cosmic mathematician'. As such,

God makes the world through a mathematical system. God's mind is constituted of mathematical propositions, and it is by His immediate creative knowledge of His own mind that He

---

26. *Human Image*, p. 33.

thinks the world into existence in accordance with this pre-
existing mathematical order. An infinite geometrical system
is the real metaphysical background of the world of nature.[27]

Sherrard's problem with Pythagoreanism, the impersonality of an
ultimately geometrical order, is repeated. To that he adds a theological objection: such a view 'means that mathematical principles
are ultimately truths superior even to God'. The consequence for
humanity is that 'mathematics ... is the sole key necessary to unlock
the secrets of nature;'[28] and that since mathematics deals in measurement and quantities, the only secure knowledge is that of the
measurable and the quantifiable.

But that, Sherrard argues, excludes most of our experience. It
even excludes the most primary sense-experience, the world as it
presents itself to us before concept and measurement begin to work.
More damagingly it excludes that dimension in which personhood
experiences itself, the dimension of value:

> We experience qualities – such as love, beauty, purpose, per-
> fection, personality, soul, aspiration and many others – that
> express value rather than quantity, and elude the net of num-
> bers. Yet according to the new scientific way of looking at
> things, such qualities cannot in fact inhere in sense-objects
> or constitute their reality, precisely because they are not
> quantifiable.[29]

It may even be suggested that such qualities are projections: 'insofar
as we experience them in sense-objects it is because we ourselves
project them on to those objects. They are actually entirely subjective, having no place in the realm of nature and no existence outside

27. *Human Image*, p. 36.
28. Ibid.
29. *Human Image*, pp. 38–9.

the individual human brain that experiences the illusion of their existence.'[30]

If that is the case, then a mathematically-governed cosmology creates another false monism, one that evades dualism simply by denying reality to elements of our experience. What Sherrard sees as denied is all that is constitutive of personhood, not only feeling but also value and meaning. Measure and quantity can never capture the reciprocity of our being, no matter how far the content of that being is falsely objectified.

IV

Sherrard continues his critique of contemporary cosmological assumptions in chapter three, 'The Apotheosis of Time and the Bogey of Evolution'. Having addressed the primacy of mathematics as the basis for knowledge, he now turns to evolution and its relation to our understanding of time.

To speak, as Sherrard does, of 'the Bogey of Evolution' is likely to ring alarm bells. Evolution, understood as the development of species by natural selection, is more than a scientific theory: it is in our times a cultural marker. On the one hand stand the scientifically informed, who 'accept evolution'; on the other, are those outside educated discourse, suspected of irrationalism. To speak of evolution as a 'bogey' arouses suspicions. And there are moments when Sherrard appears to confirm those suspicions. He speaks of 'the theory of evolution' as 'superfluous' and 'self-contradictory'.[31] In the Introduction he has contrasted pre-Renaissance models of the human with those prevalent in the modern world: 'in the great creative cultures of the world, human beings do not regard themselves as two-legged animals, descended from the apes.'[32] Is he rejecting natural selection?

---

30. *Human Image*, p. 39.
31. *Human Image*, p. 56.
32. *Human Image*, p. 4.

In part, Sherrard is being provocative. He is teasing prevailing assumptions because he wishes them to be examined. If he is rejecting anything, it is a reductive self-image: two-legged animals, ape-descended, is all we take ourselves to be. The problem is not the science but the reductive image. The real object of his critique in this chapter is evolution as a transferable structure of thought. Out of biology a model has emerged that has been generalised, is applied in quite different areas, as though its transferability were beyond question. Most relevantly for his present purpose, it has been transferred to cosmology. The 'theory of evolution', he says, 'is so deeply entrenched within current scientific orthodoxy that it is scarcely too much to say that it underpins all modern cosmological thought; to question its credibility is to question the credibility of this thought as a whole.'[33] Sherrard suspects that out of this theory has grown a false cosmology. But there seems little choice; evolution has become the standard explanatory model, and we understand things by giving an account of how they have evolved.

He sets out to explain how this situation has come about. For him, the 'theory of evolution' has its origin quite elsewhere from Darwin or natural selection. As a theory, it meets a deep need of the Western mind, one that arises from a change in the understanding of time itself. Gradually, from the medieval period, the sense of time as open to a transcendent eternity was lost. Time became empirical time, the linear time of history. 'Meaning and purpose', necessary for humanity to make sense of its existence, could be maintained only 'by attributing them in some way to the events and changes that occur in what is conceived to be a purely linear and irreversible time-dimension. Instead of these events and changes being regarded as haphazard and arbitrary, they had to be invested with an internal logic.'[34] That logic was some version of

---

33. *Human Image*, p. 56.
34. *Human Image*, p. 68.

progressive development, of evolution. Meaning and purpose had to be inscribed into linear time. 'Given the presuppositional framework to which the search to restore meaning and purpose to the processes of change and movement in the universe had to accommodate itself, it was inevitable that it issued in the theory of evolution.'[35]

Since the evolutionary model had its roots in a changed concept of time, to think about evolution is to think about time itself. Sherrard makes a distinction between a 'teleological' understanding of time and the progressive model characteristic of evolutionary thinking. Once again, he goes back to Plato and Aristotle. To speak of time is to speak of change; and to observe change in the world, as both philosophers do, is to formulate some account of time. In neither case is change taken to be simply 'haphazard and arbitrary'. Both introduce a teleology, by recognising 'final cause' as the agent of change. Plato's time, the world of Becoming, is oriented toward the forms, the archetypes, which are its final cause. Toward the forms all material being aspires. For Aristotle, too, 'changes are not haphazard or random. They do not take place according to the law of chance. They constitute a process, a development towards a certain goal. As for Plato, things in the world of nature have teleological aspirations: they aspire to realize certain potentialities.'[36] But these 'teleological aspirations' are not evolution. This aspiration does not take place along the linearity of time, because the forms and the objects are simultaneously real. Their relationship

> does not imply any theory of evolution in the modern sense; for the models according to which things in the world of nature develop from potentiality to actuality not

---

35. Ibid.
36. *Human Image*, p. 58.

only transcend this world but also form an eternal repertory, each related to the other not in any temporal sense but solely in terms of simultaneous dynamic reciprocity.[37]

Material entities take meaning from their reciprocity with the forms; meaning and purpose are realised elsewhere than within the linearity of empirical time.

Sherrard finds a parallel in pre-Renaissance Europe. The terms are different: the final cause that draws being to itself is now God. 'God is the One who eternally is and who continually draws into movement by His perfect beauty all that is potentially the bearer of a higher state of being'; draws it by what Dante calls 'the love that moves the sun and other stars'.[38] Change is accounted for; the universe is not static. But again, as with Plato and Aristotle, change and meaning arise beyond an understanding of time as a linearity of empirical moments.

With the loss of these views, Sherrard is led to speak of 'the apotheosis of time': 'one might say that in the modern scientific secular consciousness time assumes the status possessed by eternity in the spiritual consciousness.'[39] All being is now accommodated within time; all explanation must be within its terms, and those terms are necessarily mathematical, of measure and quantity. With that there is a change in the questions that humanity asks:

In this [post-Renaissance] view change is seen no longer as an expression of aspiration towards a transcendent and immortal state of being; it is seen simply as a function of mathematical structure. For the study of the *why* of

37. *Human Image*, pp. 58–9.
38. *Human Image*, p. 59.
39. *Human Image*, p. 63.

motion is substituted the analysis of the *how* of motion, and this analysis is pursued by the method of exact mathematics.[40]

Soon certain questions cannot be asked, and certain ways of understanding the cosmos are *a priori* excluded.

Sherrard has argued that a 'theory of evolution' is the consequence of the need to rescue meaning and purpose within linear time; and as such, he finds it understandable and, though erroneous, forgivable. What disturbs him is the extension of evolutionary thinking to human consciousness. First, there is the devaluation of previous states of consciousness; the thinking of the past falls out of the debate: 'Past theories about the nature of things cannot possibly provide standards or criteria for assessing the truth or falsehood of new, contemporary theories, since if they could the dogma of evolution would be invalid.'[41] 'A book like the present book', Sherrard says, 'must by definition be a non-starter', because 'it brings to bear standards and criteria of judgement' from an older, less developed human consciousness. Second, the application of evolutionary theory to consciousness undermines itself. If constant development is the reality, then the present state of awareness can claim no final authority. As by definition not the ultimate point of development,

it possesses no capacity whatsoever to pronounce on the nature of eternal metaphysical principles. It has no title even to affirm that there are such principles, much less to affirm that there is a universal law to which all things in space-time are subject. ... If the human consciousness still in the process of evolving can at one point in time escape from the

---

40. *Human Image*, p. 60.
41. *Human Image*, p. 74.

evolutionary process in order to grasp an eternal law governing the process, why not at another point?[42]

Evolutionary theory relativises human consciousness at every point;
but for humanity understood as person this relativisation cannot be
true. Consciousness changes, but the capacity to be a person, to
participate as meaning and value in that which is also meaning and
value, does not change. 'Man possesses the capacity to be totally
renewed, or reborn, at any moment of his life, and this without
there being any causal connection whatsoever between what he has
been 'in the past' and what, after such rebirth, he now is'.[43] For
Sherrard this is the defining relationship of the person to God who
is also person; and 'in God, nothing is past, nothing is future; all is
simultaneously created in the eternal now.'[44]

V

In the final part of Sherrard's critique he considers the assumptions
concerning knowledge on which modern science is based. Having
looked at the normative roles of mathematics and evolutionary
theory, in chapter four, 'Knowledge and the Predicament of Science'
he asks a more basic question: what is it that is knowable? In so
doing he moves into the area of metaphysics.

He starts with a point from the earlier chapters – that science is
not metaphysics-free. Scientists, he alleges, deny making metaphysical assumptions; their findings simply follow empirical observation.
Sherrard points out that what counts empirically is itself determined
by metaphysics; if my metaphysics allows for it, I may think I have
seen a ghost. There is also a question about what empirical experience is relevant. The scientist appeals to sense-experience:

---

42. *Human Image*, p. 73.
43. *Human Image*, p. 75.
44. *Human Image*, p. 127.

Yet this is to assume to start with that sense-experience is the sole, or at least the cardinal mode of conscious experience which is relevant to acquiring evidence as to whether a thing or a hypothesis is true or at least plausible ... In addition to sense-experience ... we possess at least two other major modes of conscious experience—those of the imagination and the emotions.[45]

The empirical goes beyond what is recordable and measurable. Nor is sense-experience self-validating. Sherrard recalls Descartes's exercise in radical doubt: 'I could consider myself not to have any hands, any eyes, any flesh, any blood, not to have any sense, while falsely believing that I possess all these things.'[46]

The primacy of sense-experience as the source of truth is, for Sherrard, itself a metaphysical position, and one that cannot be demonstrated in its own terms. Demonstrations are of course offered, and they are likely to be mathematical; but that mathematics can be the ultimate validator of truth is itself a metaphysical assumption. But, if metaphysics is unavoidable, how do we choose? Or are all metaphysical systems simply structures of our own contriving, fictions that allow some grasp on the world?

Sherrard must find a foundation. He starts by looking at reason. Since at least the seventeenth century reason has been the 'cognitive faculty' of the West, best able to deliver truth, but reason itself lacks any certain foundation. All rational argument must start from a specific point, from some premiss; 'without such a given initial proposition or premiss the reason cannot operate.'[47] That premiss though cannot be demonstrated from within its own argument. It remains

---

45. *Human Image*, p. 80.
46. *Human Image*, p. 80. Sherrard appears to be quoting from Descartes, but no reference is given. Descartes undertakes this radical doubt in his *Meditations on First Philosophy* (Paris: Michael Soly, 1641).
47. *Human Image*, p. 82.

prior, must simply be accepted for the argument to begin. It is, in reality, metaphysical. Sherrard is even prepared to see that as a matter of faith:

> Since such an initial assumption is not intrinsic to the reason, transcends proof, and is something that each human being has to accept and acknowledge – again whether consciously or unconsciously – as a condition of being able to think or reason at all, it follows that its acceptance and acknowledgement represent a personal act of faith.[48]

Science is no exception; its rationality, too, is condemned to start from such a trans-rational point of departure.

If reason cannot provide metaphysical certainty, what can? Stating a conviction that goes back at least to the 1950 lecture on St Symeon, Sherrard insists that 'there must be in man an organ of conscious experience that transcends the reason and that is capable of knowing these realities in a direct manner.'[49] He appeals again to Plato:

> Plato calls this higher organ of conscious experience the *nous* – the intellect; and the *nous* possesses a noetic power – a power of *noesis* (intellection) – through which it may intuit the realities of the intelligible world and hence grasp those principles in the light of which alone any true knowledge is possible.[50]

In that way, Plato claims, human beings can come to an intuition of the forms, the metaphysical source of all being. Such knowledge is direct and certain, and not the product of reason; it is very close to

---

48. *Human Image*, p. 83.
49. *Human Image*, p. 86.
50. *Human Image*, p. 87.

what Sherrard has called 'gnosis'. He finds a parallel in the Neo-Platonists and in the Greek Fathers, and quotes St Gregory of Sinai: 'A right view of created things depends upon a truly spiritual knowledge of visible and invisible realities. Visible realities are objects perceived by the senses, while invisible realities are noetic, intelligent, intelligible and divine.'[51] He comments: 'There is [here] the same recognition of a cognitive organ in man – the *nous* or the *intellectus* – through whose deployment he can come to know and experience ... the intelligible or spiritual world.'[52]

It is through the exercise of this capacity that, for Sherrard, metaphysical certainty is to be attained. Only on the foundation of such metaphysical certainty can the rest of knowledge, including scientific knowledge, be secure. His case is clear; but there are difficulties, not least with the terms he uses. To posit an 'organ' for spiritual knowledge verges on the circular. How can we have spiritual knowledge? Because we have an organ for it. How do we know that we have that organ? Because we have spiritual knowledge.

There is a problem here; and it arises in part from Sherrard's wish to respect premodern thought, Plato and the Greek Fathers. He is too ready to embrace their terms. His main claim, nevertheless, is what it has always been: that the human capacity for knowing extends beyond the limits imposed by the epistemology of modern science. We know things in other ways than through the application of reason or the scientific method or mathematics. Some of that knowledge is immediate and pre-rational, more recognition than deduction: we know beauty when we see it; we know goodness when we experience it. Such knowledge can indeed compose a metaphysics. Rather than recruit Plato's concept of *nous*, Sherrard might have been better served by Plato's understanding of

---

51. *Human Image*, pp. 89–90.
52. *Human Image*, p. 90.

knowledge as recollection, as *anamnesis*: that which we know, we have always known; and knowing, in its immediacy, is a recovery of what is already there.

VI

So far, in *Human Image: World Image*, Sherrard has reviewed the foundational elements of what he regards as the prevailing meta-physics of the West. In so doing he is moving toward a metaphysics of his own, one that draws from the tradition of Greek Patristic thought but is nevertheless distinctive in the centrality it gives to personhood, divine as well as human.

before setting out his own position in the final chapter of the book, Sherrard devotes two chapters to two twentieth-century cos-mologists – the French Jesuit priest and palaeontologist Pierre Teilhard de Chardin (1881–1955), and the Polish-Lithuanian poet, dramatist and diplomat Oskar Miłosz (1877–1939). Sherrard shows serious interest in both; both are attempting to restore a unified vision, to heal the cognitive gulf that opened in the West in the thirteenth century, but there is a contrast. Teilhard de Chardin, a working scientist, is motivated by a desire to close the gap between science and religion, whereas Miłosz is a visionary, a poet, a shaper of imagined worlds.

Sherrard is by no means unsympathetic to Teilhard de Chardin. He understands what Teilhard is trying to do: he is trying to heal the rift between revelation and the empirical. This rift has placed those who 'still possess some allegiance to religious values' 'in an impossible situation':

On the one hand their practical activities and, generally speaking, their thought conform to modes which have little to do with any religious understanding or purpose. On the other hand they confess to a belief in God and to the mysteries of His revelation. The result is that they are led to resolve – or to try to resolve – this schizophrenic state by tacitly separating religion from their living and their practical affairs.[53]

Teilhard tries to find a new synthesis, and Sherrard understands the pressure to do that. He sympathises, too, with Teilhard's wish to engage with the life and thought of the world; the Church must not 'turn [its] back on the world and the natural sphere of human endeavour'.[54]

He finds serious grounds for disagreement, chiefly Teilhard de Chardin's acceptance of the evolutionary model and of the linearity of time. Teilhard was, scientifically, a palaeontologist. Not surprisingly, his thinking was dominated by the idea of evolution, and his cosmology grew out of that. For him, change in all its forms, material as well as spiritual, was characterised by increasing complexity, and out of that grew consciousness. With that a new level of being appeared, what he called the 'noosphere'. That process had to have a terminus: all being, material and spiritual, was moving towards its own completion, to what Teilhard called the 'Omega point'. There, the material and the spiritual, the earthly and the divine, would become one.

The 'Omega point' was the end of cosmic evolution, the ultimate fulfilment of all change; but it was also Christ. For Teilhard de Chardin all change was intrinsically ordered towards Christ, the Logos of creation. It was that Christocentric goal that made change, including human history, meaningful. Whereas in the medieval view God was the final cause of movement toward his being, in Teilhard de Chardin's metaphysics the dynamic of change is an efficient cause, and that is evolution.

Much here might be expected to engage Sherrard's sympathy. Teilhard's cosmology does not reduce truth to mathematics. It places

---

53. *Human Image*, p. 104.
54. *Human Image*, p. 105.

Christ as Logos at the centre. It sees all human activity, spiritual as well as scientific, as part of a single movement toward a final transcendental fulfilment. Sherrard concedes much of that:

> One can see how Teilhard can recognize in [Omega] an essentially Christian phenomenon, and in fact identify it with the Christian Saviour and so achieve that reconciliation between the evolutionary and Christian perspectives which he is so anxious to realize. Given the attributes with which Teilhard has invested Omega, the transposition from the one to the other is not difficult to make.[55]

What this cosmology tells us, Sherrard suggests, is that 'God creates, fulfils and purifies the world by uniting it organically with himself', by assuming 'the control and leadership of what we now call evolution'.[56]

Around that last point a rift begins to open. Evolution, as far as we can conceive of it, requires linear time; earlier in the book Sherrard has set out his objections. Here, he raises a specifically theological problem. Teilhard de Chardin's's cosmology appears to defer the full vision of God to the end of time; it makes that vision dependent on the evolutionary advance of the 'noosphere'. It appears to make God's full revelation dependent on the processes of evolution, and so upon movement through time. However, that is to apply a human understanding of time to God, for whom 'nothing is past, nothing is future; all is simultaneously created in the eternal now.'[57]

There are further difficulties. Teilhard de Chardin's vision shifts the emphasis from the individual to the collective: it is the whole of humanity that realises its fulfilment at the Omega point. Further, it implies that human personhood is a function of evolution, of the

---

55. *Human Image*, p. 117.
56. Ibid.
57. *Human Image*, p. 129.

appearance of the noosphere, and that it is a developing process: full personhood is reached only in Christ at the Omega point. For us to be human full personhood must always be available, at every point in time. If Incarnation is the reality of all human existence, it is an eternal moment, not to be mapped on to linear time and always already complete:

> Christ is not only Omega; He is also Alpha, 'the same yester-day, and today, and forever'; and if He wishes to work the miracle of His Incarnation in all his creatures, this is not because He is in any need of completion – how could God ever be incomplete? – but because Incarnation is an essential mode of His Being and a manifestation of His original glory. In Christ, creation is already transfigured.[58]

Teilhard de Chardin's error is that he has introduced a scientific model, that of evolution, into a Christian cosmology. Had Teilhard's vision been teleological in the sense that Sherrard has already defined, had he argued that Christ was the final cause of all change, then Sherrard might have been more accepting. But because Teilhard wishes to connect science with faith he makes an essentially scientific idea, that of evolution, the driver within time of all movement towards God.

VII

In chapter six of *Human Image: World Image*, Sherrard turns his attention to another twentieth-century cosmology, that of Oskar Miłosz, and his response to this cosmology is more favourable, despite Miłosz's ideas being often obscure and even bizarre.[59] As was

---

58. *Human Image*, pp. 125–6.
59. The poet, dramatist and diplomat Oskar Miłosz (1877–1939) was Polish, born in what later became Lithuania. He spent much of his life in France and wrote in French. At the time of the Paris Peace

the case with Teilhard de Chardin, Sherrard is drawn to Miłosz because he senses a common concern:

> What he attempted to do was to diagnose why the spiritual universe of western man – essentially and inevitably, he thought, a Christian universe – had been shattered and man himself ejected into a kind of infernal void. ... [O]ur spiritual personality – our true being – cannot be actualized unless the way in which we represent to ourselves the physical universe and man's place in it accords with things as they are in reality.[60]

For Miłosz, as for Sherrard, cosmology and anthropology are dependent on each other; without a true view of our own nature there can be no true cosmology, and vice-versa.

Miłosz begins, nevertheless, from a rather unexpected question: it is not 'what am I?' but 'where am I?' His question is about the situatedness of humanity; the human subject comes to know what it is in part by knowing where it is. Western culture has given its answer: 'in time and space'. For Miłosz that prompts another question, a characteristically surprising one: 'where is space?' In asking that, Miłosz is searching for an ultimate situatedness: place not as physical location but as metaphysical reality. We have not helped ourselves, he says, by turning time and space into metaphysical absolutes when they cannot provide the ultimate placing that humanity needs. Space and time, understood as infinite extension, provide no location, do not situate the human. He speaks of 'an infinity of darkness'.[61]

Conference in 1919 he was the official representative of the newly independent state of Lithuania. He was an older and distant cousin of the better-known poet and winner of the Nobel Prize, Czesław Miłosz.

60. *Human Image*, p. 132–3.
61. *Human Image*, p. 134.

Yet, Miłosz insists on the reality of all that there is in space and time. He has no sympathy with those who suggest that the world is a function of our own perception. That we are real, that there are things, that there is a world that we can see and talk about, can be understood only in relation to space and time. However, that requires a true understanding of space and time. For Miłosz, neither has existence apart from matter, from the objects of the world: matter requires space, matter requires time. The cosmos is therefore a single 'space–time–matter' reality in which matter has priority. That can be understood only through its origin in movement. Without the movement of material things, without the changing relationships between them, there would be no space; and without movement there would be no time, because without change there would be no time. Matter, generative of both, is also the embodiment of both: all existing things concretise space and time. This provides Miłosz with a profoundly unitary understanding of being, one that connects with Sherrard's struggle against dualism:

> Manifestation – the physical universe – is thus a movement in which space, time and matter are identical. This movement is one, because it is space and time apprehended in matter. Matter is consequently itself one, like that by virtue of which it is matter – and it is matter by virtue of movement. A single movement is the unalterable matter of space and time.[62]

Miłosz has established the primary elements of his cosmology, but having placed movement at the beginning, he is faced by the problem of the source of movement. At that point his cosmology becomes a cosmogony, an account of how the cosmos came about. In a highly mythological narrative, he recounts the emergence of movement and of space–time–matter from God. In that narrative,

---

62. *Human Image*, p. 140.

light and blood are central.[63] But the essential point for Sherrard is that Miłosz is describing creation as the 'exteriorization' of God's being. In the language of this cosmogonic myth, 'in instantaneity God "exteriorizes" Himself in non-corporeal light',[64] to begin the process of the concretisation and materialisation of the world. This foreshadows what Sherrard will have to say about creation 'ex nihilo' in his final book: God does not act upon anything external to himself, not even upon nothingness. The world is already there as potential in the being of God, a potential looking for its material form.[65]

There are other points of affinity between Miłosz and Sherrard. They share a common intellectual ancestry, that divergent tradition that Sherrard describes as 'the other mind of Europe'. Miłosz, like Sherrard, draws from 'Pythagoras and the Pre-Socratics, Plato, the initiates of Alexandria, the Neoplatonists of the Middle Ages, the Christian Mystics', not to mention Boehme, Swedenborg and Goethe.[66] Miłosz shares Sherrard's intellectual ambition: he tried to develop a cosmology that would raise human knowledge to the level of 'true science, the passionate and loving science of the Divine'.[67] There is in Miłosz, as with Sherrard, an intense effort towards the expansion of the knowable beyond the mathematical limits of science. More decisively, though, both place the person at the centre of their cosmologies. For Miłosz as for Sherrard, cosmology was not abstraction; all knowing, for him, was of the person: 'Miłosz was anything but an abstract impersonal philosopher. He considered

---

63. Coincidentally, or perhaps not, Sherrard had written to George Seferis of 'this dialectic of blood and light which is the history of your people' in a letter of March 1950 (*Blood and Light*, p. 136).
64. *Human Image*, p. 142.
65. Sherrard's full discussion is in chapter 10, 'The Meaning of Creation *ex nihilo*', in *Christianity: Lineaments of a Sacred Tradition* (Brookline, MA: Holy Cross Orthodox Press, 1998), pp. 232–44.
66. *Human Image*, p. 145.
67. *Human Image*, pp. 145–6.

that all thought, all art, all science not generated out of love and prayer, and not baptised and confirmed in inner experience, was a defamation of life and intelligence.'[68]

VIII

That centrality of the person emerges with full clarity in the final chapter, 'Notes towards the Restitution of Sacred Cosmology'. Though fewer than forty pages, it holds more of Sherrard than any other comparable piece. There is his continuing struggle with dualism. There is his frustration with the Christianity of the West. There is his conviction that the scientific revolution fatally narrowed the Western mind. Most importantly, there is a radical cosmology that refuses to express itself through abstractions, that insists that persons are key to the knowledge of being as a whole. Sherrard's ambition is clearly expressed at the start:

> What is required ... is a kind of mystical-intellectual knowl-
> edge of God and divine realities that is not confined to the
> subjective inwardness of personal experience and can be
> translated into a knowledge of the world and of the cosmos
> that illuminates every object and every form of being. In this
> way what may begin as an interior and even other-worldly
> experience of spiritual realities is extended to embrace the
> whole cosmos, and to provide the life-blood of an integral
> cosmological vision.[69]

Sherrard is expressing a desire that is very close to what he had spoken of in a letter to George Seferis more than forty years before, when he said that the point was 'not to retreat before the objects of the outside world, but to *cross over them* by an extension of con-

---

68. *Human Image*, p. 144.
69. *Human Image*, p. 147.

sciousness, so that they are included within the spirit'.[70] In 1949 and in 1992 he is rejecting the idea of an uncrossable gulf between inwardness, where personhood finds itself, and the materiality of the universe. What begins 'as an interior' – our knowledge of ourselves as persons – is to be extended 'to embrace the whole cosmos'.

In approaching that goal, his language is necessarily mythological, 'the sacred mythology of the Christian tradition'.[71] The argument must begin with the relationship between God and creation. Sherrard claims that in the West, at least since the thirteenth century, the doctrine of creation has been treated as a distinct issue, apart from the doctrines of the Trinity and of Incarnation. As Incarnation was increasingly limited to the historical figure of Christ, so the idea that all material being is Incarnation was lost; creation became separate, a quasi-autonomous reality apart from the being of God. Deprived of divine presence, materiality was devalued, even seen as the enemy of spirit. Nor was this just a Western failure. Unusually, Sherrard takes St Gregory Palamas to task: he 'reiterates the depressive notion that all phenomena other than human are soulless (*apsycha*) and mindless or irrational (*aloga*)'.[72]

Sherrard insists that 'independently of the historical and individual manifestation of the Son of God in Jesus of Nazareth, the Logos already knows, and continues to know, manifestation and materialization in the cosmos as a whole, in both man and nature.'[73] But the Logos is person, one of the three of the Trinity. It is not an abstract demiurgic force, because it has its being within the *perichoresis* of the persons of the Trinity, each distinct (the Logos is not Father, not Spirit) but each drawing its being from the mutuality of the three. Since the Logos, the source of creation, is person, all

---

70. Sherrard's letter to George Seferis from London, 6 January 1949. *Blood and Light*, p. 82.
71. *Human Image*, p. 147.
72. *Human Image*, p. 149.
73. Ibid.

being, material as well as spiritual, begins in personhood. Insofar as Sherrard's cosmology requires a demiurgic force, an agency between the pure being of God and the materiality of creation, he finds it in the *Ayia Sophia*, the Holy Wisdom, that female figure who is with God at every moment of creation[74] and is itself a person rather than simply an instrument:

> The only science of nature worthy of the title is one that induces an understanding of the reality of this divine presence. ... It is one that helps us to discover not what obscure or unconscious force produces things, but what divine thought, or image, or idea, unfolding in the spiritual world, is at work in each of them. ... Each sensible thing has its own personal *logos* and *sophia* by which it is constituted, and it is this *logos* and *sophia* whose perfection is individuated in each object of the senses or the intellect.[75]

The loss of an understanding of creation as rooted in the personal inwardness of God makes creation an act of God *ab extra*: God, standing outside creation, produces something other, not himself.

That for Sherrard has become the conventional understanding in the West, and it has had profound consequences. God becomes a force not a person, and almost an antagonistic force:

> The encounter between God and man is envisaged not as an encounter between the individual human being and a spiritual presence that is the true personal subject of that being. It is envisaged as an encounter between the individual human and an inaccessible, transcendent, non-individuated God.[76]

---

74. Proverbs, 8:30.
75. *Human Image*, p. 152.
76. *Human Image*, p. 151.

There, for Sherrard, lie the roots of the alienation of the West from Christianity: 'man feels himself to be at the mercy of a single, undifferentiated omnipotence from which all men are equidistant'. The Church becomes a 'religio-socio collectivity, which, rather than trying to unite each person with his own spiritual essence, attempts to impose a kind of abstract, totalitarian, unilateral monotheism upon everyone'.[77] To see God and creation as set apart, and so in implicit opposition, is the root of dualism. If all being has its source in personhood, then a unifying vision becomes possible. Sherrard is insistent that there is only one world, not two, with no separation between earth and heaven. We live in the only world there is, one unified by God as its personal source. All being exists in *perichoresis* with that source: 'nothing less than this mutual inherence and coherence – than this interpenetration – is adequate to explain the real self of each created thing, for this is the true setting of each created thing.'[78]

Questions, however, remain. If God does not create the world *ab extra*, as a reality distinct from himself, how does he create it? And if it is not in some sense distinct from himself, surely everything becomes God, creation becomes unreal, and pantheism is the necessary conclusion? Sherrard's answer to the first question, about how the world is created, is a critique of the doctrine of creation *ex nihilo*. Though the point of that was to guard against the idea that there might be something outside of God, some primal materiality that God shaped and moulded, in practice it makes the same mistake. It erects a *nihil* outside of God. Yes, the *nihil* is no-thing, deficient in any created reality; but to place God alongside a pure deficiency is still to set something beside him in a cosmos in which he is only one part. The traditional formulation creates a dualism of its own:

---

77. Ibid.
78. *Human Image*, p. 153.

It defeats its own purpose; for it then establishes itself, or is established, as if it were positing a *nihil* – a nothing – that is totally outside God, that represents a total voidance and deficiency of God. As a consequence it introduces a dualism similar to that which it was intended to guard against.[79]

This is an issue that Sherrard takes up at greater length in chapter 10 of *Christianity: Lineaments of a Sacred Tradition*, but the question of how creation might come to be remains.

Sherrard rejects the idea that creation might not have been; the idea that God had a choice, one he exercised in favour of creation but might not have done. It is said traditionally that God creates 'entirely out of His own free will', and that to defend against the idea that God was under some external compulsion. To speak of God's 'free will' is to suggest that he might have acted otherwise and that creation was no part of his being:

> He could equally well be what He is without creating. But what is not a necessary aspect or consequence of God being what He is, is something adventitious, gratuitous and even a kind of appendage. And what is adventitious, gratuitous and a kind of appendage must be exterior to God ... and the dualism [of God and creation] is endorsed.[80]

Sherrard's answer is to speak of creation as inherent in God's nature: 'the creative act has its adequate and sufficient ground in God's Being', and 'so is an essential and necessary self-determination of that Being: that God creates the world means that he could not not create it. The divine creative act belongs to the fullness of divine life, without any mechanical necessity or outer compulsion.'[81] The act of

---

79. *Human Image*, p. 153.
80. *Human Image*, p. 157.
81. Ibid.

creation emerges from what is 'already' there in God's being. In creation he fulfils what he 'already' is:

> Creation of the world is not a gratuitous extra. It is the expression of divine life with all the power of necessity, with all the absolute freedom and spontaneity of God's Being. God *qua* God is Creator and Creator *qua* Creator is God: creation is intrinsic to His very life, it is the inner landscape of His own Being.[82]

IX

Sherrard has set out the essence of his cosmological position. God and creation are not external to each other. God does not create a material world from the outside, as something apart from himself. Rather, creation flows from the being of God; to be Creator is what God is. In the act of creation God fulfils his own being, but he also brings about a mode of being that has its own reality, that is not simply a part of him. Since what is brought into being has its origin in the Logos, in that divine person, then all being has its existence in a mutuality of personhood, in the *perichoresis* that unites all persons with their personal source. It is there that the true being of humanity is to be found.

The final and most demanding section of this last chapter is Sherrard's cosmogony. His cosmology has described what might be thought of as a steady state, the relation between God and creation. A cosmogony, an account of origins in mythic language, offers an account of a process, of how that state came about. The problems of constructing such an account are obvious. First, myth may be taken as description. Those who try to relate the first chapter of Genesis to the evolutionary history of the world make that mistake. The second problem is more radical and, strictly,

---

82. Ibid.

insuperable. A cosmogony gives an account of a process, and a process implies time. But time is part of what is created within the process; before creation there is no time, and so no time in which the process might take place.

Cosmogonies, because they are temporally constructed Narratives, are to that extent intrinsically false. But narrative and temporal process are the only language we have. Sherrard seeks to deal with that by saying that all that he speaks of occurs in simultaneity; that though the stages of his account are distinct, there is no lapse of time between them. Unlike earthly processes, creation happens in one act. The relationship between the stages is more like a logical connection than a temporal sequence: each stage is required for all the others. When one is there, all are there.

In describing how creation arises from the being of God, Sherrard sets out three stages. In the first, he thinks of the being of God in itself, absolutely single, without differentiation; what the Greek Fathers called the unknowable essence. But Sherrard is ready to ascribe to it potentiality, and that potentiality is for differentiation. He makes use of the idea (from Dionysius the Areopagite) of the Divine Names. The Names are within God – they are Names of God – but they are many and they carry the potential for differentiation. The primal differentiation, the first Names, are the three persons of the Trinity: Father, Son, Holy Spirit.

There are other Names, part of God's being but also the Names of all that comes to be in creation. We are such Names, differentiated from God but inextricably grounded in God's being, in its potential for differentiation. It is here that Sherrard begins to speak of a process. One of the Names, the Logos, gives form to all the potentials for differentiation within God himself as the ideas of what might be (of trees, stars, human beings). Here Sherrard is once again Platonic. These ideas-within-God, brought forth by the Logos, are the archetypes of creation, what Plato called forms. Already in the Logos they have a reality of their own; but as differentiated forms, as the realisation of the Names, they are the substance of all the differentiation which is to come in creation.

That is the second stage. The third stage, the concretisation of the archetypes in the material world, Sherrard ascribes to the Holy Spirit. From the Logos, the Spirit takes the archetypes and gives them life and beauty. But he cannot achieve that movement from archetype to concrete reality by himself. Sherrard proposes a working-together of the Spirit, the one who broods upon the waters, and a feminine reality, one that receives the action of the Spirit and brings forth the world. This he identifies as the *Ayia Sophia*, the Wisdom of the Hebrew tradition, the 'she' who was with God at the time of creation; but also with the Theotokos, Mary, the mother who received the Spirit and bore Christ.

For an age that does not think in terms of myth this will seem strange. But its truth lies in the relationships it embodies. The process is never mechanical; it is personal, realised by the Names that are also persons. For Sherrard this means that the very texture of being as we experience it is personal.

Rather than being onlookers on a mechanical universe, observing what is profoundly alien to us, our being as persons is the key to all that is. The most profound dualism – our being set against all else – is overcome as we recognise the interpenetration, the *perichoresis*, of our being with the ultimate Being of all. But this interpenetration is true of all being, not just our own. Only from a recognition of that will the ecological crisis, Sherrard's passionate concern in his 'Introduction', properly be addressed. It is here that Sherrard completes his search for the sacred. The sacred is not some extra, some quality added to things as they are; it is the mutuality of all being with Logos as person. That recognition allows Sherrard to say, as he does in a later essay, 'everything that lives is holy'.[83]

---

83. Originally the title of a lecture given by Sherrard to the Temenos Academy in 1994. The lecture was published as chapter 9 of *Christianity: Lineaments of a Sacred Tradition* in 1998.

8

Christianity and Transfiguration

Philip Sherrard's last book, *Christianity: Lineaments of a Sacred Tradition*, was published in 1998, three years after his death.[1] It is a collection of essays on a variety of themes which, taken together, offer an image of Christianity. His scope is broad: there is attention to the past, to tradition, as well as to the present and the future. More directly than in his previous writing he speaks of the changes needed if Christianity is to recover its position as the spiritual foundation of the West.

Sherrard, though, is not narrowly concerned with Christian definition. There is a recognition of spiritual truth on a broader scale, one that extends to non-Christian traditions. At several points the influence of Buddhism seems detectable. There is, in touching on all traditions, an emphasis on contemplation. But central to Sherrard's delineation of Christianity is transfiguration. That, for him, is a reality in the life of the individual, not a deferred possibility or a scheme for the transformation of the world. For that to take place there must be a true understanding of who we are as human beings.

---

1. Philip Sherrard, *Christianity: Lineaments of a Sacred Tradition* (Brookline, MA: Holy Cross Orthodox Press, 1998). Referred to subsequently as *Christianity: Lineaments*.

The question about ourselves leads back once again to metaphysics and cosmology.

I

A large part of this final book develops the cosmological theme already established in *Human Image: World Image*. Three of the chapters discuss modern cosmologies, in the manner of Sherrard's earlier discussions of Teilhard de Chardin and Miłosz. The five world views he engages are a strangely-assorted group. Together with Blake, Nietzsche and Jung, there is the fifteenth-century Byzantine Platonist Gemistos Plethon [2] and the twentieth-century French metaphysician and esotericist René Guénon. [3] Again, the issue, as with Teilhard de Chardin and Miłosz, is how adequately they place humanity within the totality of their view. As before, he respects these figures for attempting an overall vision, something that contemporary culture has largely abandoned. He also uses them as points of contrast to clarify his understanding of Christianity.

The longest of these discussions is chapter four, 'Christianity and the Metaphysics of Logic'. Its focus is double: primarily René Guénon, but also the Hindu tradition of Vedanta on which Guénon drew. He was a thinker from the margins, and Sherrard may to some degree identify with that; but he admires him for his ambition. He sees Guénon as having given an impetus to a largely lost tradition of narrative cosmogony, which for Sherrard is an important part of metaphysics. 'If during the last century or so there has been even some slight revival of awareness in the western world of what is

---

2. Giorgios Gemistos Plethon (*c.*1360–1450), lawyer, theologian and Platonist, was a representative of the Orthodox Church at the Council of Florence in 1439.
3. René Guénon (1886–1951) was born in France, raised a Catholic, but later took on Egyptian nationality and as, a Muslim, was known as Abdalwahid Yahia. He devoted his life and extensive writings to Hindu, Taoist and Buddhist thought and to esotericism generally.

186

meant by metaphysics and metaphysical tradition, the credit must go above all to Guénon'.[4] Yet he admits that there must be reservations. Guénon was the object of 'misplaced adulation', and his writing displays errors of information and areas of ignorance.

Both Guénon and the Vedanta begin from an uncompromising assertion of the unity of the 'Absolute', understood as 'the sum total of Reality'.[5] For Guénon the Absolute is also to be understood as the Infinite, and he sees the Infinite as universal possibility. Sherrard summarises: 'the Infinite is also universal possibility – the All-Possible. Hence it is the idea of the Infinite ... that constitutes for Guénon the supreme metaphysical principle, the Absolute that in its turn constitutes the primordial datum of his doctrinal exegesis.'[6] If this Absolute is infinite possibility, what (if anything) is impossible? Guénon has an answer: 'for Guénon, an impossibility is an absurdity in the logical sense of the word. The absurd, in the logical sense of the word, is what implies a logical contradiction. Conversely, it is the absence of internal contradiction which *logically as well as ontologically* [my italics] defines a possibility.'[7] Guénon makes a logical test, the absence of contradiction, the limit to the possible and so a limit on Infinity and the Absolute. What is logically possible comes to equate with what is ontologically possible. What fails that logical test, what reveals internal contradiction, cannot be.

Sherrard has problems with this argument. It might at first sight appear to be the difficulty he raised in his discussion of Teilhard de Chardin: that to see some abstract process such as evolution as the motive power not just of the universe but of God's purposes is to make God subject to something pre-existing. In the case of Guénon, the 'pre-existing' would be the rules of logic. Guénon seems to be

---

4. *Christianity: Lineaments*, p. 76.
5. *Christianity: Lineaments*, p. 99.
6. *Christianity: Lineaments*, p. 79.
7. *Christianity: Lineaments*, p. 80.

saying that God cannot do anything that offends against logic and so makes a contradiction. Sherrard does not quite make that accusation. He admits that logic, for Guénon, does not govern the Infinite; but at the same time 'there is nothing in the metaphysical order that cannot be expressed in terms that conform to the laws of logic because, for Guénon, anything that cannot be so expressed is an impossibility'.[8] There is 'a strict correlation between the order of logic and the metaphysical order'.[9] If not by governance, God seems to be restricted by a strict requirement.

Sherrard, however, has a deeper objection, one that is rooted in the theology of the Trinity as understood by the Greek Fathers. They acknowledge the essence of God, but they also affirm the persons of the Trinity. The essence is unknowable and 'beyond determination and differentiation'; the persons, however, are differentiated, Father, Son and Spirit. But this does not make the persons other than the essence, determined in a way the essence is not: the essence has its being in personhood, and the persons have their being in essence. Neither essence nor persons have priority. 'Just as there is no non-hypostasized [non-personal] Essence, so there are no non-essentialized Persons.'[10] Yet essence and persons can be distinguished, can be spoken of separately.

Logically that amounts to a contradiction: we distinguish entities that, in their being, are not distinguished. That for Guénon could only be a logical absurdity, an impossibility. But the Trinity is foundational for Christianity. If the Trinity cannot be accommodated within the rules of logic, Christianity has to admit, in those terms, contradiction and paradox. But what for Guénon would be an absurdity and so ontologically impossible is for the Christian to be accepted as the paradoxical nature of the divine, as being that is in its own nature non-contradictory but not subject to our rules of logic.

---

8. *Christianity: Lineaments*, p. 82.
9. *Christianity: Lineaments*, p. 83.
10. *Christianity: Lineaments*, p. 84.

That therefore it is an antinomic and paradoxical idea in the sense that from the logical point of view it does not conform to the law of non-contradiction, is not something arbitrary or due to a lack of logical subtlety and refinement on the part of Christian exegetes. *It is imposed on them by the way in which the Absolute has been typified for them by divine revelation.* That is to say, the Absolute has revealed Itself to be essentially paradoxical in character.[11]

Possibility, in Guénon's logical sense, cannot be the test; for Sherrard, the possible may extend to what, to the human mind, is absurd.

Sherrard has other difficulties with Guénon. One has to do with the reality of the material world. For Guénon, the 'most real' is the Absolute, from which everything springs: its possibilities are 'completely and totally real in themselves'.[12] Two questions arise: how do these possibilities pass over into the 'manifest' world, the world we experience? And what reality does that world have? To bring about a world of material particulars some determination must be at work. Guénon insists that, compared with the reality of the Absolute, the 'determined state of a universal possibility is [Sherrard quotes Guénon] "rigorously nothing".' The implication is that Being, all that comes to be, is "rigorously nothing"; our world is an unreal shadow of what exists in the Absolute: 'any doctrine which places the sum total of reality outside and above not only phenomenal existence but also Being itself is bound to reduce Being, and, *a fortiori*, phenomenal existence to a kind of insignificant shadow.'[13] But Sherrard has always insisted on the full reality of our world.

What does Sherrard take from his struggle with this strange figure? He is drawn to someone who asks these kinds of questions;

---

11. *Christianity: Lineaments*, p. 86.
12. *Christianity: Lineaments*, p. 95.
13. *Christianity: Lineaments*, p. 96.

and he wrote a fuller and more sympathetic account of Guénon in a late uncollected essay.[14] There he agrees with Guénon's insistence that 'spiritual knowledge' is of little use without a practice, a discipline that is the initiation into that knowledge. In this last book, though, Guénon's use is chiefly as a foil for the 'lineaments' of Christianity. He starts from an abstraction, the Absolute or the Infinite. For Sherrard, Christianity does not start from an abstraction; it is not a theory of the universe. It begins from persons, the persons of the Trinity, and persons are not abstractions. It is because we can relate to those persons that we can be persons ourselves, not the abstractions of some anthropological theory. Sherrard also finds Guénon guilty of undermining the reality of creation. Christianity in Sherrard's understanding insists that the world we see is fully real, is no shadow. Only on that basis does Incarnation make any sense. Christ does not enter our world as an illusion into illusions.

Sherrard raises similar points in his discussion of the Hindu tradition of Vedanta. Here there is an even purer version of the primal unity of all being. In this system the principle is *advaita*: all duality is denied. There is only one reality, and distinct existences are an illusion. We find ourselves in a world of distinctions and differences, of individualities; and there must be a question as to how that, even as illusion, comes about. The primal unity must be the source; but how in a cosmos of absolute unity can there be any becoming? Sherrard offers an interpretation: 'in the extreme form of the *advaita* the answer is that ultimately nothing becomes; the world does not exist, or is but the appearance of *māyā* (neither being nor non-being).'[15] This means that our own existence is illusory, and the point of a spiritual discipline is to help us realise that. 'The creature *qua* creature can have no concrete or eternal destiny', it exists in 'a state of bondage' to illusion, 'total deliverance from which is only

14. Philip Sherrard, 'The Universal Tradition', *Indian International Centre Quarterly*, 14 (2), 1987, pp. 5–20.
15. *Christianity: Lineaments*, p. 101.

possible on condition that it ceases to exist as a creature in any and every way whatsoever'.[16]

Against Vedanta, Sherrard's commitment to dualities, to the reality of distinct existences, is again apparent. For him, it is Christianity that secures that. His final objection to such a system, and to all the cosmologies of absolute unity in which no distinctions of being are possible, is simply experiential. The spiritual projects that such systems offer are a contradiction of life as it is lived:

> The notion, implicit in the concept of non-duality, that it is possible for us to realize in this present life our essential identity with the supra-personal Absolute, and thus to attain a state in this present life in which ... we ourselves are impervious to vicissitude and error, is not one that is valid in the Christian view of things; for in this view everyone, whatever the degree of perfection he or she has attained, is still exposed in this present life to both these contingencies. To think otherwise is, in this view, to ignore the mystery of human freedom, inalienable whatever the state of grace we may have been granted.[17]

II

In chapters five and six of *Christianity: Lineaments of a Sacred Tradition* Sherrard continues his indirect delineation of Christianity, this time by considering those who have despaired of it and attempted to construct some replacement. The thinkers in view are Gemistos Plethon, Nietzsche, and Jung; and in the background, as often with Sherrard, hovers the figure of Plato. Again, as with Guénon, there is an undercurrent of sympathy with these figures, however much Sherrard may in the end disagree with them.

---

16. *Christianity: Lineaments*, p. 105.
17. *Christianity: Lineaments*, p. 113.

Gemistos Plethon is the least familiar. Born in Constantinople in the last years of the Byzantine Empire and aware of the Muslim threat, he made an attempt to heal the schism in Christianity of the eleventh century. He sensed the dualism that had entered Christianity from the time of Augustine: this was a dualism that saw the world as fallen, corrupt, the place of sin, infinitely removed from the divine realm. His response was to turn back to Plato, to draw on an ancient unifying vision.

The detail of Gemistos Plethon's position is unclear; his chief work, the *Laws*, was burnt by the Patriarch shortly after the fall of Constantinople in 1453. Nevertheless, he seems to have found in Plato's universe of interpenetrating form and matter a healthful corrective to the Christian position. For Gemistos Plethon,

> Christianity, in embracing or appearing to embrace a dualism which radically separated the world of the senses from its transcendental origin and by focusing attention almost exclusively on the historical redemption of man, had broken the great tradition of the ancient world. It had broken the myth of this tradition which had linked the visible cosmos to its invisible archetypes.[18]

Against that he 'sought to link every aspect of life with the divine through the whole chain of being'. Sherrard places Plethon in the line of descent of 'the other mind of Europe'; his antecedents include Pythagoras as well as Plato and the Neoplatonists, and his successors Marsilio Ficino, Giovanni Pico della Mirandola, Giordano Bruno and the Cambridge Platonists of the seventeenth century.

Gemistos Plethon was looking for another way, one that would circumvent the insoluble theological conflicts that had split

---

18. *Christianity: Lineaments*, p. 128.

Christianity and made the Christian world vulnerable to the threat from the east. He spoke of a new religion, one based on the best thought of the ancient world.

He is reported to have said at the Council of Florence that 'both Christianity and the Moslem faith would soon be superseded by a religion not greatly differing from that of the ancient Greeks.'[19] Sherrard, for his part, says very little in the way of direct dissent. Instead, he allows Plethon to stand as a witness for the prosecution against a dualistic form of Christianity that rejected the full creatureliness of humanity, its physical being in a material world. If Sherrard makes any argument against Plethon, it is that he abandoned the Christian tradition too readily.

Gemistos Plethon attacks the implicit dualism in Christianity; and Sherrard sees Nietzsche as the culminating expression of that response: 'it was with Nietzsche that the full force of this reaction developed.'[20] Nietzsche, however, traced the endemic split between spirit and body beyond Christianity and back to the Greek philosophers. He saw Socrates and his successors as the decadence of a tradition. Summarising Nietzsche, Sherrard says:

> These philosophers represent [for Nietzsche] a revolt of the reason against the instincts. They establish an absolute morality set over against life. They teach the immortality of the soul, a doctrine of the Beyond, and a denial of the senses. They turn their back on the world, and thus prepare the way for Christianity.[21]

Sherrard agrees with Nietzsche in finding the moment of truth in ancient thought, 'not in the fifth century BC ... but in the sixth

---

19. *Christianity: Lineaments*, p. 117.
20. *Christianity: Lineaments*, p. 128.
21. *Christianity: Lineaments*, p. 139.

century, and even earlier'; in the 'age of Dionysos', a 'period of the affirmation of life'. He quotes from Nietzsche: in that age there was 'a yea-saying without reserve to suffering's self, to guilt's self, to all that is questionable and strange in existence itself'.[22] Sherrard's sympathy is clear:

> It was this unity of life and its acceptance as a whole, for itself, with no question of a Beyond or of any purpose other than that which is fulfilled in its affirmation in spite of all contradictions and illogicalities – it was this that the later philosophers destroyed when they elevated the reason to a position of supremacy over the instincts and elaborated a morality derived from the reason which in itself can never escape from the dualist attitude.[23]

He agrees, too, with Nietzsche that Christianity was central to these dualisms: 'it had split creation in two and had disrupted those ties which link man to the universe. ... It had waged war on the body and on man's eroticism.'[24]

There is an echo here of Sherrard's argument in *Christianity and Eros*. However, he goes on to qualify his agreement. Just as Plethon abandoned Christianity too soon, so Nietzsche ignores the material aspect of Christianity, its sacramental investment in the physical creation, which presupposes 'an understanding of things entirely at odds with that which [Nietzsche] sees as endemic to the Christian mentality'.[25] Broadly, though the accusation stands. Whether from Nietzsche's perspective or that of Gemistos Plethon,

---

22. Sherrard (*Christianity: Lineaments*, p. 129) is quoting from the Appendix to Friedrich Nietzsche', *The Birth of Tragedy* (first published in German by E. W. Fritzsch, 1872).
23. *Christianity: Lineaments*, p. 129–30.
24. *Christianity: Lineaments*, p. 132.
25. *Christianity: Lineaments*, p. 133.

Christianity has failed to affirm 'the transcendent One and the changing multitudinous world of the senses' as a 'single, undivided and indivisible reality'. Sherrard, however, is not looking for a monism of the Absolute. There is a task for contemporary theologians: to create a theology that is 'capable of embracing and validating the integral reciprocity of the two poles of life – the transcendent and the immanent, the One and the many, the intelligible and the sensible',[26] to do justice to duality without creating the conflicts of dualism.

Sherrard's third interlocutor is Jung. As with the others, there is little direct argument; most of the essay is exposition, But that does not conceal Sherrard's position. He begins by quoting Jung's dismissal of metaphysics: 'all conceivable statements ... are made by the psyche. ... The psyche cannot leap beyond itself.'[27] Sherrard rejects that as a truism: of course all human statements arise from the psyche. But its intention is to deny the possibility of metaphysics; and that Sherrard rejects.

His essay is entitled 'Christianity and the Religious Thought of C. G. Jung', and the first question is whether Jung's thought can be considered religious. His dismissal of metaphysics might seem to demand a negative; Jung is looking for a spiritual *tabula rasa*, and, like Gemistos Plethon, for a new basis for the spiritual life. That was to be found in observation and the theory of the psyche. Sherrard suggests that Jung 'regarded himself as the apostle of a new religion, one that should replace for western man the exhausted formulas of Christianity'.[28] He refers to Jung's dream of God dropping a large turd on the cathedral of his hometown and shattering it. God had 'disavowed' the religion of the Church, and something had to

---

26. Ibid.
27. Sherrard is quoting from C. G. Jung's autobiography, *Memories, Dreams, Reflections* (London: Pantheon Books, 1963), p. 322 (*Christianity: Lineaments*, pp. 135–6).
28. *Christianity: Lineaments*, p. 138.

replace it; and it was Jung who 'had been entrusted by God with this mission'.[29]

What this mission involved, Sherrard suggests, was made clear by another of Jung's dreams – that of a phallus on a throne in an underground cavern. Christianity had cultivated a spiritual abstraction, an ideal; it had ignored or excluded the dark of humanity. Consequently, Sherrard says, 'we had failed, through traditional Christianity, to overcome or escape our anxiety, bad conscience, guilt, compulsion, unconsciousness and instinctuality [stet].'[30] Not only were those elements of the human requiring necessary recognition, but for Jung they were also elements of God himself. Christianity had foisted all that on the devil; but 'the devil is also God. God is "the dark author all created things, who alone is responsible for the sufferings of the world".'[31]

Jung may have been reacting, Sherrard suggests, to a narrow and moralistic Protestantism, to the faith of his father, but he was also rejecting 'the rationalism of current nineteenth-century scientific thought'. Both sought to keep the world and experience at arm's length: this entailed using rationalism by constructing a 'two-dimensional conceptual world in which the reality of life is well covered up by so-called clear concepts', faith by building a hedge of belief that kept the world at bay. Sherrard quotes Jung: 'the arch sin of faith, it seemed to me … was that it forestalled experience'.[32] In place of faith and reason Jung appealed to the unconscious, individual and collective, 'a kind of repository of all those psychic elements and drives which have either not entered man's conscious world, or been driven out of it'.[33]

---

29. *Christianity: Lineaments*, p. 139.
30. *Christianity: Lineaments*, p. 140.
31. Jung, *Memories*, p. 97 (in *Christianity: Lineaments*, p. 141).
32. Jung, *Memories*, p. 98 (in *Christianity: Lineaments*, p. 142).
33. *Christianity: Lineaments*, p. 144.

Among the several problems Sherrard has with Jung the most significant is that he wholly internalises the spiritual life. The human task has to do with the psyche; individually and socially, the spiritual objective is the recovery and integration of all that has been hidden or unacknowledged, relegated to the unconscious. If there is a God for Jung, it is the integrated psyche. Jung's religion, if it is to be called that, 'is a religion of pure psychic immanence'.[34] The idea of a relationship with God is rendered unnecessary; God himself, in any traditional sense, is unnecessary.

Nonetheless, there are feature of Jung's thought that Sherrard admires. There is his rejection of rationalism; there is also his acceptance of myth. Sherrard summarises his view of Jung by saying that 'the main lines of his thought, his central concepts and images, constitute what really amounts to a theology and a mythology';[35] and it is significant that he respects the mythology of Jung's dreams. Perhaps most important is that he finds in Jung a thinker attentive to experience. Against a Christianity that has often ignored experience in favour of doctrinal abstraction, it is from the experience of the psyche that Jung begins. He questions how faith works in actual lives, how it often excludes experience. There is in Jung

a plea for man to face the realities of his own inner world, to take his own path in the fulfilment of his personal created destiny, and not to barricade himself, as is so often the case, behind an abstract structure of religious or metaphysical principles whose only real function is to prevent him from ever realizing who or what he is, to prevent him from ever developing the potentialities of his own unique being.[36]

---

34. *Christianity: Lineaments*, p. 154.
35. *Christianity: Lineaments*, p. 140.
36. *Christianity: Lineaments*, p. 155.

III

Sherrard has presented a group of figures whose ideas, acceptable or not, help him to clarify his view of Christianity. His discussion of Guénon and the Vedanta underlines his rejection of any metaphysics of an impersonal absolute. Plethon offers a Platonic god who is impersonal and remote. Nietzsche and Jung expose a main failing in Christianity, its inability to acknowledge the fullness of what it is to be human; but they do not offer the metaphysical dimension of the 'other world' that Sherrard has insisted on since his early correspondence with George Seferis.

The main contribution of this last book to Sherrard's cosmological understanding is the tenth chapter, 'The Meaning of Creation ex *nihilo*'. This takes up an argument that began in the last chapter of *Human Image: World Image*. There he had criticised the traditional formulation, which, in trying to avoid the suggestion that there was something apart from God from which he created the universe, in practice posited such a something: the *nihil* from which God made all being. Although the *nihil* was nothing, what resulted was an original doubleness of being: God, but also nothing.

Sherrard attempted to escape that difficulty by proposing that creation was already there as a potentiality in the being of God, that the created universe *is* the being of God in the mode of time and space. As a potentiality within God's being, God fulfils himself in the act of creation; that for God not to create would have been for him not to be fully what he is. Sherrard repeats his position in the seventh chapter of *Christianity: Lineaments*, the chapter entitled 'The Presence of Evil: Christian and Neoplatonic Views': 'God cannot not love: to love is a necessity of His being what He is. Similarly, God cannot not be the Creator: to create is a necessity of His being what he is.'[37]

For Sherrard, this overcomes the dualism between God and creation. The traditional formulation, creation *ex nihilo*, implies an

---

37. *Christianity: Lineaments*, p. 165.

external act: God acts on the nothing to bring about material reality. That externality sets God apart from the being he creates. But Sherrard's account leaves him with another problem, one that seems to have presented itself more forcefully after the writing of *Human Image: World Image*. That is the problem of evil. If creation existed as a potential in the being of God, then evil too must have existed in the being of God. Jung's belief that such is the reality seems to have prompted further thought; and Sherrard refers to Jung's inclusive good-and-evil image of God at the start of chapter seven, 'The Presence of Evil'. He reviews some of the main attempts to account for evil. One is the Platonic opposition of Being, pure and eternal, to matter as its temporal degradation, and hence evil. Another is the view that any descent from perfection, from that of the forms or of God, involves imperfection, and that imperfection either equates with evil or is an opening for it.

In the end Sherrard finds himself coming back to what might be described as the free-will theory of evil. If creation were an emanation of God himself, entirely continuous with his being, it would be perfectly good as God is good. But Sherrard insists on the duality: there is God, and there is creation, and each is real in its own terms. To allow creation reality must be to allow it freedom. And it is in the exercise of freedom that evil arises; we have the choice to act badly.

Sherrard is aware that this by no means solves the problem. Questions remain: is evil a reality or simply a deficiency of the good? Is it possible that creation might have existed without evil? To these he attempts answers; but his more interesting response is in chapter ten, on creation *ex nihilo*. There he introduces an understanding of the being of God that goes beyond that of *Human Image: World Image*, one that opens the possibility of a meeting with, not just the ideas of Jung, but those of non-Christian traditions.

He begins by suggesting the harm that the traditional *ex nihilo* doctrine has done in the West; it is in this very doctrine that the dualism of the Western mind began. Previously, Sherrard had traced

that dualism to the Aristotelian revolution in medieval Western theology. It was Aristotle's negation of the Platonic link between
material entities and the transcendent forms that led to empiricism,
to the rational analysis of an autonomous material world. Now he
finds a deeper root. If the *nihil* is conceived of as nothing, as pure
void and non-being,

> if the world is created out of nothing conceived of in this
> purely negative and privative sense, it must be created out-
> side God. For clearly this nothing is not a quality of God's own
> nature and reality – on the contrary, it is entirely privative of
> God. Nor can it ever become a quality of God's own nature and
> reality in such a way that it could be said that there is a natural
> relationship between God and the nothing. Hence the world
> that is created out of this nothing must exist outside God.[38]

This view – that the world does in fact exist outside God – has become
the normative view of the West, the root of modern alienations.

What can Sherrard say to correct that? He goes back to Patristic
theology and to a different understanding of *nihil*. In St Gregory of
Nyssa the statement that 'God created the world *ex nihilo*' appears,[39]
but the *ex nihilo* is read differently. For Gregory, the *nihil* is not 'an
absolute blank', 'an entirely negative category':[40]

> On the contrary, it is a positive category. It denotes the
> absence of all space, time and matter, or of everything exten-
> ded in space and time – the absence, that is to say, of all that

---

38. *Christianity: Lineaments*, p. 237.
39. For creation *ex nihilo*, Sherrard refers to authors such as Gregory of
    Nyssa, Eriugena, and the *Corpus Dionysiacum*. Professor Andrew Louth
    has pointed out that the latter cannot be appealed to for this purpose
    and suggests that Sherrard's particular interpretation of *ex nihilo* is not
    to be found in any of these sources.
40. *Christianity: Lineaments*, p. 238.

can be called a 'thing'. ... It may be envisaged as the fathom-less, incomprehensible ground or depths of God's uncreated energies and possibilities, the pre-ontological 'nihil' from which all things proceed. In this way it refers not to some-thing that is outside or privative of God, or that is void of His presence. It refers to what is within God.[41]

This develops Sherrard's creation theology in the final chapter of *Human Image*: what comes to be is already there in the being of God. But now the *nihil*, the nothing, is to be found there too, not as an external entity. 'The original act of creation is that of the differen-tiation of the forms of all things from the undifferentiated unknow-able ground – the *nihil* – of the Divinity.'[42]

Previously, Sherrard has spoken of the potentialities contained in God's being; following the Pseudo-Dionysius, he described them as the Divine Names, and in Platonic terms as the archetypal forms. Now he is willing to say that there is in God that to which the word 'nihil' may be applied: there is absence, there is even a divine empti-ness. Sherrard is uncomfortable with Jung's suggestion that evil may have its root in the being of God; but the *nihil* is not to be read as evil. There is in the unknowability of God that which can only be called *nihil*, because it 'precedes' differentiation, is nothing created. At that level the distinction between being and non-being vanishes. This idea, suggestive of a divine emptiness, perhaps relates to the Buddhist idea, that the absolute of being is an infinite, but infinitely compassionate, emptiness.

IV

Sherrard's attempt to construct a cosmology provides the frame for his account of Christianity. It is striking, though, that his presentation

---

41. *Christianity: Lineaments*, p. 239.
42. *Christianity: Lineaments*, p. 240.

of Christianity is very much set in the context of an investigation of religious traditions generally, almost to the point that the word 'tradition' becomes the most important consideration. Again it is clear that, vital though Orthodoxy is for Sherrard, it stands for him within a broad perspective of human spirituality. This is apparent in the first chapter of the book, 'The Meaning and Necessity of Sacred Tradition'. Here he sets out his principal requirement – a spiritual framework for human life that reveals its mutuality with its transcendent source.

To find that, Sherrard looks beyond Christianity. He asks the question: 'what is it that distinguishes cultures that retain a grasp on life which we appear to have lost?' Is there some 'element' that they have that is missing in contemporary culture?

> If we are to judge from the art of these civilizations we are bound to say that there is. For whether we speak of the art of the ancient Greek world, or of the art of India, or of the Islamic world, or of our own Christian world down to the time of the Renaissance, it is of a religious art that we are speaking. It is an art, that is to say, dedicated to the expression or revelation of realities that are more than human or natural, realities that we denote by the word 'spiritual'.[43]

These 'realities' Sherrard would describe as metaphysical; but it is not in that form that human beings relate to them. In those other cultures, Greek, Indian or Islamic, there are narratives and rituals that make spiritual realities a matter not of concept but of experience. Sherrard turns again to myth: 'The religious myths that underlie the cultures in which we recognize the presence of some quality that now eludes us are, for the people of such cultures, not mere human inventions but symbols and images that make possible a direct and constant intercourse with the universal principles of

---

43. *Christianity: Lineaments*, p. 2.

life.'[44] Yet, the modern world has lost that: 'a whole language of the soul, a whole spiritual science, has been lost to us'. Those who live in such cultures do more than believe; their images and symbols are not confined to rites and temples. They 'paint them on their pottery, weave them into their clothes, sing of them in their songs, dance in obedience to them'.[45] Their lives are suffused with an awareness of its spiritual source.

It is that which has been lost in the contemporary world. What is already clear is that, for Sherrard, Christianity, as one tradition among many, draws from the same source. Spiritual 'realities' are available to all human beings in the varying forms of different traditions. As he says later in the book, 'the Church as a whole must renounce the claim that the Christian revelation constitutes the sole and exclusive revelation of the universal Truth.'[46] The essential point is not doctrinal correctness; any valid spiritual tradition has to be realised in experience, in the detail of life.

Yet, traditions are needed because they offer a necessary spiritual discipline; the spiritual life cannot be a matter of personal taste, of making a cult from whatever suits. Sherrard's openness to the various traditions is not a version of the *philosophia perennis*, with its tendency to generalise away the specifics of tradition, to create an insubstantial universalism of intention and feeling. He questions the esotericism that often characterises such a position:

This other-worldly type of esotericism only too often degenerates into a kind of spiritual debauchery, in the sense that it has its counterpart in the idea that it is possible to cultivate the inner spiritual life, and to engage in meditation, invocation

---

44. *Christianity: Lineaments*, p. 3.
45. Ibid.
46. *Christianity: Lineaments*, p. 51.

and other ritual practices, whether consecrated or coun-
terfeit, while our outward life, professional or private, is lived
in obedience to mental and physical standards and habits that
not only have nothing spiritual about them but are completely out of harmony with the essential rhythms of being,
divine, human and natural.[47]

A spiritual life must be a life; it must include the outward as well as
the inward, living as well as contemplating. That connection is what
all the major traditions maintain, and that is the discipline.

Sherrard's most direct discussion of the relation between the
different religious traditions is in an uncollected essay from 1974,
'The Tradition and the Traditions'.[48] By 'the Tradition' he means a
postulated universal truth from which all traditions derive, a
central core of wisdom in the light of which all historic religions
might be judged. He accepts that all traditions would affirm that
there is such a truth, that truth must be one. But he argues that we
have no way of knowing that truth, because we all, necessarily, start
from within a particular tradition and judge from within it. There
is consequently no possibility of formulating a universal religion;
the all-encompassing *philosophia perennis* is, by implication,
impossible:

> The claim to speak in the name of the Tradition, whether one
> calls it 'universal' or 'metaphysical' or 'primordial', whose
> principles allow one to interpret and resolve the conflicting
> viewpoints of the various traditions, must be treated with
> considerable care. One must not forget that the idea of a uni-
> versal religion, or the proposition that 'all truth is one', in itself

47. *Christianity: Lineaments*, p. 227.
48. Philip Sherrard, 'The Tradition and the Traditions', *Religious Studies*, 10
    (4), 1974, pp. 407–17.

neither resolves the question of 'which tradition enshrines the most truth' nor establishes their equal authenticity.[49]

For Sherrard, the more immediate reality is that all traditions provide a discipline, an initiation into the spiritual life, and need to be accepted on those terms.[50]

The traditions are important. Nevertheless, Sherrard sees religious exclusivism as a false response to the need for tradition. In the first chapter of *Christianity: Lineaments* he rejects the Latin exclusivism of Boniface VIII, his bull *Unam sanctam* of 1302. 'We are bound to believe in one Holy Church' outside of which there is 'neither salvation nor remission of sins'.[51] For Sherrard, 'Christianity stood in the line of a tradition of wisdom and knowledge whose historical appearance is long prior to the advent of Christianity.'[52] He rejects the use of the word 'pagan' for the pre-Christian world. He mentions Heraklitos and the mysteries of Eleusis, Samothrace and Lemnos; he speaks of the similarities between those mysteries and the early Christian cult. He points to initiation. Just as the mysteries required rituals of initiation, so did Christianity: 'one has to recognize that in its essential form Christianity is an initiatory religion that is in many ways similar to the Mystery-religions of the pre-Christian world.' Like them, it held a secret truth: there was a *lex arcani*. He mentions Origen, who 'explicitly speaks of secret doctrines that can be taught only to the initiated'.[53]

Not for the first time Sherrard characterises Christianity as an esotericism; as well as properly describing what he takes Christianity

---

49. Ibid., p. 471.
50. Sherrard offers essentially the same arguments against the possibility of a stateable *philosophia perennis* in a later uncollected essay, 'The Universal Tradition', *Indian International Centre Quarterly*, 14 (2), 1987, pp. 5–20.
51. *Christianity: Lineaments*, p. 51.
52. *Christianity: Lineaments*, p. 28.
53. *Christianity: Lineaments*, p. 29.

to be – initiation around a mystery – that links it to older and broader traditions. In the first chapter of the book, and in language that hints again at a parallel with the ancient Mysteries, he speaks of 'initiation into the contemplative state'.[54] Within Christianity that initiation is the Eucharist; the Christian is one who has been initiated into the Eucharistic mystery. When he speaks of the Constantinian conversion of the empire, he laments a loss: in becoming a state religion Christianity suffered a diminution. Hidden, secret and persecuted, it had been truer to itself.

At such points Sherrard is mainly thinking of Christianity as a social reality, of its place in the public sphere; what had been a personal initiation around a mystery inclined, with the conversion of the empire, to a normative public obligation. However, he argues that in its essence Christianity cannot admit an esoteric–exoteric dualism. In the second chapter, 'Christianity and Christendom', he insists that Christianity takes seriously the public as well as the private, the open as well as the hidden. The manifest, the world of creation, *expresses* the hidden: 'it is the expression of the non-manifest in the manifest, of the absolute in the contingent, of eternity in time, of the One in the many.' That removes any barrier between the esoteric and the exoteric. Christianity is not a withdrawal into a secret truth; it 'cannot be indifferent to the most profane aspects of the social order, or the world. Its concern is not with flight from but with the transfiguration of the world.'[55] Sherrard is attempting a difficult balance. Christianity looks for the transfiguration of the human sphere; in that sense it is open, inclusive, not secret, but the heart of that transfiguration is inward; it is the initiation of each person into the mystery, which is secret.

Sherrard turns from viewing Christianity alongside other traditions to that inwardness. At the heart of his account of Christianity

54. *Christianity: Lineaments*, p. 17.
55. *Christianity: Lineaments*, p. 31.

is contemplation. Just as God did not make the world 'ab extra', so the life of the spirit cannot be lived from the 'without' of dogma and ethical rule. 'Sacred tradition in the highest sense consists in the preservation and handing down of a method of contemplation.'[56] This is true of all traditions; they are disciplines of instruction, modes of cultivation of the inwardness of contemplation. For Sherrard, this is the only way we can step beyond 'our bodily, psychic and merely ratiocinative life' to attain 'knowledge of and communication with the Divine'.[57] Again there is a link with the ancient world; that is how the injunction, 'know thyself', is to be understood:

> What the Delphic injunction proclaims ... is that a condition of achieving human dignity is that we give priority to contemplation and gnosis – to follow a contemplative and gnostic way – for contemplation is the action through which we are led to a knowledge of our true identity and hence of the true identity and being of other things as well.[58]

Yet the balance of inner and outer must be maintained. Sherrard is clear that contemplation always takes place within the structure of a tradition. In Christianity that structure is formed around revelation.

Sherrard's understanding of revelation is hardly a conventional one. Revelation is generally understood as the divinely authenticated statements of the Church, the public creedal formulations, whereas contemplation is personal, private, even secret. Sherrard detects a dualism. For him revelation is what is known in contemplation; the contemplative state is not an empty state. Something is known that is not known by the empirical mind, and it is that which is revelation. Sherrard speaks again of archetypes. In 'The Meaning of Sacred Tradition' he moves from that Platonic shorthand to a fuller account

---

56. *Christianity: Lineaments*, p. 11.
57. Ibid.
58. *Christianity: Lineaments*, p. 246.

of what is known. It is an intuitive and immediate knowledge, but it has nothing in common with 'intuition as it is understood by philosophers like Bergson or by writers like D. H. Lawrence'. For them

> intuition is a purely instinctual and subconscious faculty that lies beneath the reason and not above it, and has its source in impressions received through the body and the senses, and in feelings and images aroused in us by the experience of our physical being and our subjective emotional reactions to them.[59]

Whereas empirical knowledge is divisible into elements – knowing this depending on that, knowing this in contrast to that – the gnosis of contemplation has no elements: it is a single knowledge of one thing, and that is being as an epiphany of God. That is its content, that is what is known; but not as an object of knowledge, rather as the state in which the knower is. 'We come to realize that we are the epiphanic form of a divine archetype. At the same time we come to realize that each visible reality is the epiphanic form of the Divinity. We come to perceive God in all things.'[60]

That, however, is not the final state of contemplative knowledge. The contemplative intellect transcends the first level of vision, and 'from seeing God in all things ... comes to see all things in God':

> So far, looking towards the many or the realm of multiplicity, the intellect has come to perceive in each of all these things a spiritual quality or dimension, seeing each as the manifestation of the Divine. Now it has to transcend the realm of multiplicity, not by rejecting what it now perceives, ... [but] by realizing ... that all are the flower and growth of one root.

---

59. *Christianity: Lineaments*, p. 16.
60. *Christianity: Lineaments*, p. 17.

Thus the intellect is led back from the many to the One and sees all things as one in the One, from whom all multiplicity derives.[61]

What was a unity of knowing is now a knowing of unity.

A question arises: how does this knowing relate to the empirical knowing of the rational mind? Sherrard finds an answer in some words of St Maximus the Confessor, in the relation between experience and concept. The knowing of contemplation takes priority over concept, takes place in an area not governed by concept:

> The immediate experience of a thing suppresses the concept which represents the thing. I call experience knowledge in act which takes place beyond all concept. I call intuition the participation itself in the object known, at a level above all thought.[62]

Contemplation is participatory knowledge; in it the opposition between knower and known is overcome. It is not hard to see why in Sherrard's search for a unifying vision contemplation was central. Developed and disciplined within a spiritual tradition, it was how humanity could come closest to a vision of all that is.

V

Gnosis, the knowledge that flows from contemplation, transforms the individual, yet it also touches the common world of relationships with others. In the final essay Sherrard gives an account of how contemplation flows into action. He has been speaking of hesychasm, the practice of silence and inward prayer that is the contem-

---

61. *Christianity: Lineaments*, p. 18.
62. C. Laga and C. Steel eds (2018) *Maximus Confessor: Quaestiones ad Thalassium* (Turnhout, Belgium: Brepols, 2018), quoted by Sherrard in *Christianity: Lineaments*, p. 7.

plative tradition of the Orthodox Church. He describes the gnosis of contemplation as a 'state of recollectedness' that fulfils our nature: 'true human nature is "recollection of God" – recollection in the ontological and Platonic sense of *anamnesis*, a "remembering", that implies direct participation in an immanent divine principle.'[63] Our knowledge of ourselves is transformed and we are transformed, and from that flows action and the good. 'To act well, we must first know. Thus, while contemplation and action are complementary, they are not on an equal footing: contemplation must precede action. Correct action depends on a correct mode of being: without being good, we cannot do good.'[64] The route to right action is not a matter of ethical rule; it lies through the change that the life of contemplation brings. He finds that in the early history of Christianity. Initially, the Church had no programme for 'the christianizing of society'. 'Originally, Christianity possessed no legislation applicable to the social order, nothing which corresponds to the *shariyah* of Islam.' The early Church was a 'society within a society, again like the pre-Christian mystery religions'.[65] It had no power to legislate for or control the wider society. Its focus was on the transformation of the individual life; any positive act, any good that flowed to society flowed from that transformation. But with the conversion of the empire the scope for action changed. Now it could entertain the ambition of transforming the whole; and with that came a shift to moralism. For the imperial Church and its successors,

> the quantitative and collective becomes more important than the qualitative and personal. That the faithful should lead good Christian lives in moral terms (which means in obedience to the laws and institutions of the Church) is regarded as of more concern than the initiation of the few into the

63. *Christianity: Lineaments*, p. 247.
64. *Christianity: Lineaments*, p. 246–7.
65. *Christianity: Lineaments*, p. 31.

mysteries of the Kingdom of God; and the well-being of the whole Church regarded as a single corporate entity is of more concern than the well-being of any one of its individual members.[66]

Contemplation leads to knowledge, and knowledge leads to action, but Sherrard has more to say. Alongside the word 'gnosis' he places another word, '*agnosia*' 'unknowing'. This is, first, the clearing away of the mass of empirical knowledge that clouds the contemplative vision. But he is also suggesting that which is found in many mystics, Western as well as Eastern: that the knowing of contemplation moves beyond itself to become what can only be described as 'unknowing'. At that point the knowing reaches towards the essence of God in its absolute unknowability; towards that from which everything knowable, even God himself, is a descent.

If contemplation requires a clearing through the accumulation of empirical knowledge, on the larger scale Sherrard sees the necessity of a clearing away of much that has inhibited and paralysed the Western Church. It is striking how much in this final volume is critical of contemporary Christianity, of the common assumptions and many of the self-understandings of the Church in the West. The thinking of the Greek Fathers feeds him, but his image of Christianity is not just backward-looking. His account has implications for the future; and at several points in this book he sets out what needs to be done.

In 'Christianity and Christendom' (he echoes Kierkegaard's distinction without quite repeating it), Sherrard summarises his long-standing diagnosis of the problems of the Church in the West, of a Church that became an imperial institution and subordinated 'its essentially initiatory and contemplative purpose' to those of doctrinal rectitude and moral control. Its focus shifted from

---

66. *Christianity: Lineaments*, p. 36.

transformation to ethics; the Christian society was defined in moral terms and the path to it was moral action. Just as the idea of evolution gave meaning to change in linear time from which transcendent meaning had gone, so bringing about a Christian society gave meaning to a Church that had lost the goal of individual transformation. The project of social improvement inevitably moved to secular institutions (Sherrard mentions the European Community). The Church continues to 'bear witness' through its liturgical life and through 'personal sanctity and prayer', but its real purpose has gone. 'The Church simply stumbles along at the heels of the world, adopting ideas and practices entirely alien to it but which in spite of it have shaped the dominant forms of our contemporary society. The truth is that the Church is profoundly in bondage to secular culture.'[67] And that culture fails to feed us. Sherrard's frustration explodes: 'it is impossible to live a human form of life in a world that lacks meaning, that lacks reality, that imprisons us within a welter of artifacts of an ugliness and banality that defy description.'[68] The Church has been complicit in the making of such a world. It has become 'little more than a social institution of Christian welfare oscillating between extremes of senile protection, modernism, and effete imitation; with a teaching of vague, ill-assorted and eviscerated theological notions compounded with negative moral precepts.'[69]

Nevertheless, Christianity is the only spiritual resource that the West has. It is from that 'sacred tradition' that any recovery must begin. Sherrard is quite blunt: 'we can only emerge from the terrifying blind alley in which we find ourselves by refounding our life on a religious basis'; and that basis must be Christianity, the religion 'that lies at the root of every significant manifestation of our culture over the last fifteen hundred years and more'. He

---

67. *Christianity: Lineaments*, p. 48.
68. *Christianity: Lineaments*, p. 49.
69. *Christianity: Lineaments*, p. 52.

mentions architecture, art, music, painting, poetry; but Christianity is there in the very texture of the land. 'It impregnates the hills and valleys of our landscape through the presences and sanctity of the saints and the holy men and women who once inhabited them.'[70]

If this situation is to be redeemed two radical changes are needed. The first is a renunciation of 'coercive authoritarianism', the Church as 'a state within a state', the sole agent of truth and salvation. The second change is inward. The task of the Church is transfiguration. That requires 'reaffirming and giving pride of place to its essentially gnostic and contemplative nature'. The good of the world depends not on some 'Christian renewal movement' but on the presence in the world of those who are transfigured 'by following the path of gnosis and contemplation – the mystical path'.[71]

VI

With *Christianity: Lineaments of a Sacred Tradition* we reach the end of Sherrard's lifetime of writing. The question must be asked: how well does this book fulfil the promise of its title?

There are problems in making that assessment. It is clear from the introductory acknowledgements that though 'the writing and compilation was completed shortly before the author's death', the preparation of the published text was necessarily the work of others. The shape of the book may not reflect the form and the focus that Philip Sherrard might have given it had he lived to oversee the process.

Then the word 'lineaments' suggests a tentative approach to the subject – outlines, a sketch rather than a full portrait. Though in some essays Sherrard enters the technicalities of Christology and the theology of creation, matters close to the heart of Christianity, the reader is left to form the outline from his discussion of what may

---

70. *Christianity: Lineaments*, p. 50.
71. *Christianity: Lineaments*, p. 52.

seem tangential issues and figures of marginal relevance. Whether that is the result of the balance of material available or a deliberate indirectness on Sherrard's part, it is hard to judge.

Nevertheless, a picture does emerge, and it is both personal and of general importance. It is necessary to recognise what does not form part of this presentation of Christianity. The figure of Jesus, and his life and teaching, rarely appear. There is no talk of an evangelical 'gospel'. Instead the words 'tradition' and 'sacrament' are central; to be a Christian is to be initiated into those mysteries. The effect is to a degree paradoxical. For someone who speaks so often of tradition, Sherrard's Christianity is minimally historical. Rather, it is present, immediate; its realities – spiritual discipline, the trans-figuring power of sacrament – are there and to hand in our world, in our time and universally available. To enter their reality is to join, not just the inheritance of St Symeon and St Maximus, but that of all humanity, touched by a radiance that flows through all traditions.

Retrospect

This study has followed Philip Sherrard through more than half a century of thinking and writing. Some questions remain. How does his work stand in its various relevant contexts? How successful was he in meeting his own demands? And why is he worth reading? There is his theology to consider, particularly his critique of the Western Church. There is his epistemology, his wish to broaden the scope of human knowledge beyond the limits set by modern science. There is his image of the human. But all are contained within his passion for a unifying vision, for the recovery of a perspective in which the fragmentation of human experience is overcome.

There is, of course, a personal context. The detail of that must await a biography. What is clear, however, is the effort of a remarkable man to make sense of the world and of his place in it. After an uncertain childhood on the margins of between-wars Bloomsbury, and after his immersion as a twenty-year-old in the horror of the Second World War, the effort began: a questioning and an exploring that continued to the end of his life. Greece provided him with a cultural world that fed him and a milieu in which his mind could flourish. With his conversion to Orthodoxy in 1956 he found a secure base, but his intellectual energy did not cease; he was never the convert who retreats behind the walls of an all-answering truth.

It is important, too, to recognise that Sherrard, for all his engagement with Greece, its language, poetry and culture, speaks very much from the West. His response to the Greek world is that of an Englishman, one born in and moulded by the Englishness of the

215

earlier twentieth century. That was his starting point. Although he chose Greece and the Orthodox Church, what he has to say is not necessarily what an *indigène* of that culture or that Church might say. There is an underlying distance that gives his work its acuity. As he said to George Katsimbalis in a letter of 7 August 1950, 'a *déraciné* Greek is almost a contradiction in terms. If he is *déraciné* he will no longer be Greek. A *déraciné* Englishman is still on the contrary English.'[1]

Perhaps the most profound effect of his openness to the Greek world is the materiality of his thinking. From his response to the substantiality of Seferis's poetry to his insistence that the material world is a potential of God's being, there is resistance to the conceptualisation of the world in science, and to abstraction, that marker of the spirituality of the West. Against the other-worldly aura of a Gothic cathedral Sherrard offers the closeness, the tactile immediacy of a village church, a small Byzantine *naos* where meaning is embedded in the stone.

I

Yet, for all his insistence on the immediate, Sherrard is a thinker of depth and complexity, and his *opus*, seen at its full extent, is primarily theological; indeed, he has been recognised as an important lay theologian of the Orthodox Church. There is, though, a larger context. Just as his Orthodoxy must be seen in the context of his Englishness, so his theology must be seen in its historical context.

The latter half of the twentieth century saw a profound change in Western culture. From the time of the conversion of Constantine, Christianity had been its spiritual, intellectual and cultural foundation. Over a period of little more than fifty years, from the 1940s to the 1990s, that ceased to be the case. Christianity became marginal, both for the mind and the life of Western Europe. That was a change

---

1. *Blood and Light*, p. 361.

at least as momentous as Constantine's conversion; after a millennium and a half, imperial Christianity, though it preserved its formal institutions, had lost its power.

Sherrard's response was to explore the inner failure of the Western Church, its inability to provide a spiritual base and its resulting alienation from thought and society. That failure was rooted in a misconception of the nature of Christianity, a recurring theme in his work from his essay on El Greco in 1950 to the final chapters of *Christianity: Lineaments* in 1998. What began as an initiatory religion of the transfigured life became a moralistic authoritarianism. He offers no scheme of renewal, but he is certain that only by a rediscovery of the contemplative tradition might Christianity once again feed the world. He does not exclude that possibility; indeed, he sees the recovery of Christian spirituality as the only hope for a world driven by the power of economics and approaching environmental disaster. The tone of his later writings is not hopeful; the world seems intent on its own destruction.

Sherrard's theology is in essence a critique of the theology of the imperial Church, of its corporatist exclusivity. He sees Christianity as needing to open itself to the wider traditions of human spirituality, from those of the ancient world to parallel traditions in the present. One of the conditions of the renewal of Christian spirituality is that the Church renounce its claim to be the sole and exclusive revelation of the universal Truth. He is ready to say that the divine Logos is as present in the spirituality of a Brahmin, a Buddhist, or a Moslem as it is in a Christian.

For him the essential is contemplation, within the discipline of a spiritual tradition. Contemplation is not, for Sherrard, a solitary and isolating activity; it is an experience of participation. Awareness of God is participation in God. In seeing the good and the beautiful we know ourselves to be part of the good and the beautiful. The dynamic of the cosmos is what he calls *perichoresis*, that is a mutuality in which being is shared, but without loss of distinction.

217

Such participation dissolves the gulf between knower and known; it is the life of relationships, between the human and the natural world as well as between the human and God.

Most crucially, the perichoresis of person with person is the condition of all personhood. For that to be a reality, Sherrard appeals to the doctrine of the Trinity. For him it is not an abstract analysis of the being of God, but the primary interchange of personhood that makes all personhood possible. Without it all relationships would be external, object with object. It is because God is known irreducibly as a person that human beings experience themselves as persons. Whereas Western churches speak hesitantly of the Trinity and are inclined to put in its place one or other of the persons – Jesus for Evangelicalism, the Holy Spirit for Pentecostalism – Sherrard insists that only by holding to the paradoxical incomprehensibility of God in three persons can human beings truly know who they are.

How useful is this theology for the present day? At first the indicators might not seem promising. It is founded, after all, in Orthodoxy, perceived in the West as one of the more conservative traditions of Christianity. Yet, from that tradition Sherrard draws imperatives that are highly relevant for Western Christianity. The first is that Christianity is about transcendence, about a transcendent God who is not to be assimilated to human purposes. It is not about moral improvement or about the perfection of society. The second is that God is not some extra to the universe, to be invoked on appropriate occasions. The third is that God is to be known in contemplation; that a Church that seeks to realise him in declaration, however 'evangelical', will always miss the point. But perhaps most important is that any religious vision must include the entirety of human experience, the material as well as the spiritual. The drift of religion in the West into abstraction, into a dematerialised realm of rarely-inspected creedal statement, must be reversed if Christianity is ever again to engage with the spiritual experience of the contemporary world.

II

Sherrard offers a critique of the theology of the Western churches; he offers an equally radical critique of the assumed epistemology of secular society. This is basic to all his arguments, to his theology, to his understanding of what it is to be human, and to the possibility of a unifying vision.

The target of his critique is the narrowing of the knowable by modern science. As early as his letter to George Seferis of 8 January 1950 he speaks of 'cold scientific intelligences', and in his last book he speaks of the loss of 'a whole language of the soul, a whole spiritual science'. This has excluded the truth to be found in myth, image and symbol. Sherrard believes that without those older cognitive resources we cannot know the truth about ourselves. Much of what is human is now passed over; feeling, the perception of beauty and love itself are relegated to the private realm of the subjective and can be known only to the extent that they become the objects of empirical science. The result, as he said in his 1950 essay on El Greco, is that we have become objects even to ourselves.

The deeper consequence of this narrowing of the knowable is the death of metaphysics. Sherrard insists that metaphysics is inescapable and that to support any ultimate meaning it must be a transcendental metaphysics. The access to such truth cannot be a matter of deduction; it depends on that immediacy of recognition that he calls 'gnosis'. His 'gnosis' is participatory knowledge, knowledge in which knower and known, though distinguishable, are joined in mutuality. Sherrard's supreme instance is knowledge of God, but this way of knowing is not exclusively theological. For him, the greatest poetry exhibits this 'gnosis', this participatory union. It is clear from their correspondence that it was Seferis's power through symbol and myth to inhabit the world he saw that drew Sherrard so strongly to him. For Sherrard, knowing in its fulness is a single act; Seferis was able see the depth without ever abandoning the immediate, the material, the earthy.

That single act, that unified vision, had, for Sherrard, to include our view of ourselves. We need to start not from some abstract theological definition – Augustine's embodied soul – but from the materiality of our experience, from what we find ourselves to be. Hence, his rejection of the tendency within Christianity to spiritual-ise ourselves, to reject the body as an inconvenient accident. Just as the material universe is not a secondary reality, unreal in that it is not God, so the bodily reality of human beings is not an accident of a fallen state. We are one, a unity not to be falsified in any body–spirit dualism.

The excessive spiritualising of Christianity, with its turning away from the body, is for Sherrard a narrowing of the knowable, as cul-pable as the scientific reduction of the human to an object, whether biological or psychological or sociological. Sherrard's unifying vision starts from a unified vision of our own being; it is that which for him opens a unifying vision of being as a whole.

III

The critique of Western theology, the insistence on a widening of the knowable, the image of the human – all these are pervasive concerns in Sherrard's work, but they fall within his larger passion for an ultimate vision of the unity of all being. It is what underlies his critique of dualism, his analysis of the medieval divorce between revelation and reason, his fierce rejection of the disjunction of body and spirit. That he came close to such a vision is suggested by the title he gave to his Temenos lecture in 1994, 'Every Thing That Lives Is Holy'. There was no true image of the human that was not part of such a vision, no faithful theology that did not begin from such an intuition of unity. Yet he lived, necessarily, in the common world of fragmentation and conflict; that is often apparent in the increasingly polemical manner of his later writing and the anger that sometimes floats to the surface. The goal, the vision, was never abandoned, a goal that, perhaps, is unachievable within a human life. For him, it was inseparable from love. In his 2003 memorial lecture, Bishop Kallistos Ware quoted some words of Sherrard's. "Apart from love", wrote Philip, "there is no reason for the existence of the world." Only if we feel what he termed an "ontological tenderness" – a loving sensitivity for "the fragilities of fern, shell or wing" – shall we be able to find a solution to the current ecological crisis.'[2] All being is worthy of love and it is love that reveals the unity of being.

Did he find that unifying vision? There are glimpses, moments when it is there on the far margin of perception but still withholds itself, but the need, the drive towards it, is never in doubt. The search begins from the brutal incoherence of the Italian battlefields. Poetry helps him, but chiefly the poetry of others. His own poetry, powerful though it often is, rarely steps beyond the fragmentation and the conflict. Particularly in the work of Seferis, he glimpses the possibility that poetry itself may, at its best, be a unifying vision, one in which the human spirit and the materiality of the world become one.

Then there was human culture and tradition. Sherrard's immediate and deep attachment to Greece grew out of a recognition that there was, in Greek culture, a wholeness of view, an organic linking of nature with the human, of the past with the present, of the body with the spirit. He sensed that in the physicality of Greece; he immersed himself in it when he chose to live in the old mining valley of Katounia. He saw it enacted in the life of Byzantium, in the cloistered life of Athos, where physical and spiritual discipline became a single act of devotion.

---

2. Kallistos Ware, Metropolitan of Diokleia, *Philip Sherrard: A Prophet for Our Time. The First Annual Sherrard Lecture at the Prince's Foundation* (Oxford: The Friends of Mount Athos, 2008), p. 13. The words quoted are from *Sacred in Life*, p. 21, and the poem 'The Dust', in *Sign of the Rainbow*, p. 140.

Most of all he looked for the single vision in faith. Against all the dualisms of the mind, against all the distinctions and oppositions that are currency of conceptual thought, he looked for a point from which thought and feeling and experience and aspiration might be one. His instinct was that of a mystic: that beyond the truths of ideas and argument there lay a nameless truth, one that words could not capture, before which words must give way. There are, in Sherrard's writing, moments when the curtain of words parts and something shows itself.

Was he successful? In that region, success is hardly the word, and if it points to anything, it is not to be exposed for public consumption. Sherrard, like most human beings, lived within words; his life is a torrent of words through to the end. In the search for a unifying vision he is a great pointer, an indicator of the way. He tells us not to assume that what we know is all that can be known. His critique of the Western mind is a critique of assumptions, of the everyday taken-as-read of science and secularism and history, but also of faith. There is a deep and productive scepticism in Sherrard's work. It is not the negative scepticism of a Descartes but one that allows something to emerge: the supposedly outworn truths of the past, the possibility of a transcendent dimension to human existence, a fullness of human being that our culture implicitly denies. That opening of the mind is Sherrard's success.

Postscript: Katounia

In 1995, towards the end of his life, Philip Sherrard built a small stone church in the grounds of Katounia, a disused mining site he had bought with a friend in 1959. He gradually restored it into a place in which to live and to which he could welcome friends. The church is small, perhaps twelve feet wide and thirty feet long; it might accommodate twenty people standing in the Greek manner. The windows are small and there is little light apart from the flames under the icons, but even when empty, it is full of presences. On the walls and arches and under the dome there are frescoes commissioned by Denise Sherrard and executed by the iconographer Aidan Hart, and the church feels full. All around stand the saints to which Sherrard felt closest – St Symeon the New Theologian, St Maximus the Confessor, St John Chrysostom, and St Gregory Palamas. Their figures support you on all sides, some holding scrolls with the words by which Sherrard best knew them. Above the main arch is the Theotokos, Mary, holding the Protecting Veil that spreads each side of her, covering all within, the living and the dead.

Although Sherrard did not see the completed work, to stand in that church is to learn something about him. He lived and thought within that company of presences. The figures on the walls were to him more than names, more than ancient texts, more than the raw material of theological study. He shared his living and thinking with them, with presences he could not deny, with those who had spoken the truth that the world could no longer hear; with an overarching presence that alone gave humanity the power to be human.

Philip Sherrard's grave in Katounia.

Around the walls, tucked into the corners of the frescoes, are animals: hares, deer, an owl, a frog. There are flowers and trees and birds. Suddenly, the world is opened; beyond human preoccupations and human wisdom, there is space. God's infinite creativity is doing what it will in its endless freedom.

Bibliography of Philip Sherrard's Work

Poetry

Orientation and Descent, with Other Poems (Eton: Alden and Blackwell, 1953).

Motets for a Sunflower: A Sequence of Twenty-two Poems (Ipswich: Golgonooza Press, 1979).

In the Sign of the Rainbow: Selected Poems 1940–1989 (London: Anvil Press Poetry, 1994).

Prose works

The Marble Threshing Floor: Studies in Modern Greek Poetry (London: Vallentine, Mitchell, 1956). Reprinted Limni, Evia, Greece: Denise Harvey (Publisher) 1981, 1992.

The Greek East and the Latin West: A Study in the Christian Tradition (London: Oxford University Press, 1959). Reprinted with a new Appendix Limni, Evia, Greece: Denise Harvey (Publisher), 1992, 1995, 2002, 2017.

Athos: The Mountain of Silence (London: Oxford University Press, 1960). Originally published in German translation, 1959.

The Pursuit of Greece (ed.) (London: John Murray, 1964. Reprinted Athens: Denise Harvey & Company, 1987).

Constantinople: The Iconography of a Sacred City (London: Oxford University Press, 1965). Originally published in German translation, 1963.

Byzantium (Netherlands: Time Inc., 1966).

Modern Greece (with John Campbell) (London: Ernest Benn, 1968).

Essays in Neo-Hellenism (in Greek) (1971).

W. B. Yeats and the Search for Tradition (Ipswich: Golgonooza Press, 1975).

Christianity and Eros: Essays on the Theme of Sexual Love (London: SPCK, 1976) Reprinted Limni, Evia, Greece: Denise Harvey (Publisher) 1995, 2022.

Church, Papacy, and Schism: A Theological Enquiry (London: SPCK, 1978). Reprinted Limni, Evia, Greece: Denise Harvey (Publisher) 1996, 2009.

The Wound of Greece: Studies in Neo-Hellenism (New York: St Martins Press, 1979).

The Rape of Man and Nature. An Enquiry into the Origins of Modern Science (Ipswich: Golgonooza Press, 1987; reprinted 1991). Reprinted Limni, Evia, Greece: Denise Harvey (Publisher), 2015.

Edward Lear: The Corfu Years ed. (Athens: Denise Harvey & Company, 1988).

The Sacred in Life and Art (Ipswich: Golgonooza Press, 1990). Reprinted Limni, Evia, Greece: Denise Harvey (Publisher) 2004, 2023.

Human Image: World Image (Ipswich: Golgonooza Press, 1992. Reprinted Limni, Evia, Greece: Denise Harvey (Publisher), 2004.

Christianity: Lineaments of a Sacred Tradition (Brookline, MA: Holy Cross Orthodox Press, 1998).

The Witness of the Poet: Perspectives and Comparisons (in Greek) (1998).

Translations

Six Poets of Modern Greece (with Edmund Keeley) (London: Thames and Hudson, 1960).

George Seferis: Collected Poems 1924–1955 (with Edmund Keeley) (Princeton: Princeton University Press, 1967).

C. P. Cavafy: Collected Poems (with Edmund Keeley) (Princeton: Princeton University Press, 1975).

George Seferis: Complete Poems (with Edmund Keeley) (London: Anvil Press, 1978).

The Philokalia (with G. E. Palmer and Kallistos Ware) (London: Faber & Faber, 1979–95).

Angelos Sikelianos: Selected Poems (with Edmund Keeley) (London: George Allen & Unwin, 1979).

Odysseus Elytis: Selected Poems (with Edmund Keeley) (Harmondsworth: Penguin, 1981).

Essays and letters

This Dialectic of Blood and Light: George Seferis: Philip Sherrard, An Exchange 1947–1971. Edited by Denise Sherrard (Limni, Evia, Greece: Denise Harvey (Publisher), 2015. Reprinted with amendments, 2023).

'The Light and the Blood.' Edited by Ari Sharon. (Letters to George Katsimbalis), *Arion* (Boston) 7 (1) 1999.

Major uncollected articles

'The Tradition and the Traditions: The Confrontation of Religious Doctrines', *Religious Studies*, 10 (4) 1974.

'Odysseus Elytis and the Discovery of Greece', *Journal of Modern Greek Studies*, 1 (2) 1983.

'The Universal Tradition', *Indian International Centre Quarterly*, 14 (2) 1987.

'Return to Immortality', *Indian International Centre Quarterly*, 16 (3–4) 1989.

Reviews of Sherrard's work

Of *The Greek East and the Latin West*:

> W. Norman Pittenger, in *Journal of Religion*, 40 (2) 1960.
> Glanville Downey, in *Speculum* (Chicago) 35 (4) 1960.
> Gervase Mathew, in *New Blackfriars*, 41 (482) 1960.
> François Masai, in *Latomus,* tome, 22, 1963 (in French).

Of *Athos: The Mountain of Silence*:

>Ernest W. Saunders, in *Journal of Religion*, 41 (2) 1961.

Of *Constantinople: Iconography of a Sacred City*:

>Gervase Mathew, in *New Blackfriars*, 47 (544) 1965.

Of *Church, Papacy, and Schism*:

>Fergus Kerr, in *New Blackfriars*, 60 (705) 1979.

>Patrick O'Connell, in *An Irish Quarterly Review*, 69 (275/6), 1980.

Of *The Sacred in Life and Art*:

>S. C. Malik, in *Indian International Centre Quarterly*, 17 (2) 1990.

Index of Names

Martin Corner was born in East Yorkshire in 1939. Educated in Birmingham, London and Portsmouth, for forty years he taught English and American literature at the Universities of Ibadan Nigeria, Copenhagen, and Kingston, and more briefly in the United States and Russia. He holds degrees in English Literature from King's College London, in Russian Studies from the University of Sussex, and a PhD in Theology from Heythrop College, University of London. He has published on a range of authors including Virginia Woolf, John Updike, Richard Ford, and Saul Bellow. After retirement he worked for ten years as a Reader in the Anglican diocese of Southwark. He is married with two children and three grandchildren. He lives in Kingston, Surrey.